ANDRE ST PIERRE

Cryptocurrency Technologies Unlocked: Bitcoin, Blockchain and the Rise of New Digital Money

How do Cryptocurrencies Work? What is Blockchain? What does the Future Hold for this Disruptive, Game-Changing Technology?

This book is dedicated to my son Xavier James St Pierre. He is a light in my life that burns bright and he shares the same craving for learning, growing and laughing that I do. By the time he reads this book, I expect that as a society, we will have progressed so that blockchain and cryptocurrency technologies will have solved many of our current, seemingly impossible global challenges.

Love you Xavier

Contents

A Quick Note to the Reader

Congratulations on the commitment you made by purchasing this book and the investment in your own knowledge and growth. You are expanding your knowledge in blockchain technology and cryptocurrencies which I believe will have an incredible impact on our everyday lives. The technology has such disruptive potential and will contribute positively to solutions in many important areas such as world-wide poverty, hunger, crime, environmental, health care, finance, space exploration, security and more.

Take your time reading this book as it covers a lot of information. There is a table of contents to refer back to chapters/notes as needed.

In addition, the technology evolves very quickly and, while all information is relevant at the time of publication (end of 2024), it is possible new developments and technology will have changed at the time of your reading. That being said, I anticipate that the fundamentals will have remained the same.

I am honored (honoured for my fellow Canadian readers) that you have chosen this book for your growth.

Happy reading and learning!

Understanding the Future of Blockchain and Cryptocurrency

In the last decade, few innovations have generated as much excitement and confusion as blockchain technology and cryptocurrencies. What started as a niche concept rooted in cryptography and digital currencies has now evolved into a powerful force shaping industries, economies, and even our understanding of trust. If you're reading this, chances are you've heard the terms "blockchain" and "cryptocurrency" thrown around in conversations, headlines, and perhaps even your social media feeds. But what do they really mean? How do they work? And, perhaps most importantly, why should you care?

In this book, we'll dive into these questions, break down complex concepts, and explore the real-world applications and future potential of blockchain and cryptocurrencies. Whether you're new to the space or looking to deepen your understanding, this introduction will give you a solid foundation.

The Basics of Blockchain and Cryptocurrencies

At the heart of blockchain and cryptocurrencies is a simple yet powerful idea: trust without the need for intermediaries. Let's start with **blockchain**.

Blockchain is essentially a decentralized, digital ledger—a database—that records transactions in a secure, transparent, and immutable way. Imagine a book where each page records a transaction, but once a page is filled, it can't be edited. The book is shared across a network of computers (also known as nodes), meaning no single entity controls the information. This makes it resistant to tampering, censorship, or fraud. It's a bit like having a public record that anyone can access but no one can alter.

Now, cryptocurrencies—like Bitcoin, Ethereum, and thousands of others—are digital assets built on blockchain technology. They are designed to serve as a medium of exchange, just like traditional money. However, cryptocurrencies differ from regular money in several important ways. Unlike fiat currencies (such as dollars or euros), cryptocurrencies are decentralized, meaning no central bank or government controls their issuance or value. Instead, they rely on the blockchain's underlying cryptographic protocols to ensure security and transparency.

Bitcoin, the first and most well-known cryptocurrency, was created in 2009 by an anonymous person or group of people known as Satoshi Nakamoto. It introduced the concept of peer-to-peer transactions without the need for banks, credit card companies, or other financial institutions. Since then, thousands of new cryptocurrencies have emerged, each with its own unique features and use cases, but all powered by blockchain.

How Blockchain and Cryptocurrency Work in Practice

Now that you understand the basic concepts, let's explore how these technologies work in practice. Imagine you want to send some Bitcoin to a friend. Here's what happens behind the scenes:

1. **The Transaction**: You initiate the transaction by signing it with your private key (a secret cryptographic code that proves ownership of your Bitcoin). You then broadcast this transaction to the Bitcoin network, where it's picked up by miners (more on them in a moment).
2. **Validation**: Miners are participants in the Bitcoin network who verify the transaction. To do this, they solve complex mathematical puzzles that require a significant amount of computational power. This process is called **proof of work**.
3. **Adding to the Blockchain**: Once the puzzle is solved, the transaction is grouped with others into a "block," which is then added to the existing blockchain. The new block is linked to the previous block, forming a chain of blocks. This is where the name "blockchain" comes from.
4. **Confirmation**: Once the transaction is added to the blockchain, it's considered confirmed and irreversible. The transaction is visible to everyone in the network, making it transparent, but because it's cryptographically

secured, it's nearly impossible to alter.

The entire process takes just a few minutes, and once it's confirmed, your Bitcoin is on its way to your friend. The beauty of the system is that it operates without any central authority. There's no bank in the middle, no government regulating the transactions—just a network of computers working together to maintain trust and transparency.

Real World Applications and the Future of Blockchain and Cryptocurrencies

While the idea of a digital currency may seem abstract, the real-world applications of blockchain technology are vast and far-reaching. Let's take a look at a few key areas where blockchain and cryptocurrencies are already making an impact:

- **Finance and Payments**: The most obvious application is in the world of finance. Cryptocurrencies like Bitcoin and Ethereum offer a decentralized alternative to traditional banking and payment systems. They allow people to send money across borders instantly, at a fraction of the cost of traditional methods, without relying on banks or payment processors.
- **Smart Contracts**: Platforms like Ethereum have taken blockchain a step further by enabling **smart contracts**—self-executing contracts where the terms are written directly into code. These contracts automatically execute when certain conditions are met, cutting out the need for intermediaries like lawyers or escrow agents. This has the potential to revolutionize industries like real

estate, insurance, and even governance.

- **Supply Chain Management**: Blockchain's transparency and immutability make it ideal for tracking goods and verifying the authenticity of products in supply chains. By recording every step of a product's journey—from farm to table, or factory to store—blockchain can help reduce fraud, prevent counterfeit goods, and increase trust in product sourcing.

- **Healthcare**: Blockchain can revolutionize healthcare by securely storing patient records and making them accessible to authorized medical professionals while ensuring privacy. Patients can control their data, and doctors and hospitals can securely share information across systems without the risk of data breaches.

- **Digital Identity**: In a world where identity theft and data breaches are growing concerns, blockchain could provide a secure way for individuals to manage and prove their identity. By creating digital identities on the blockchain, people could have more control over their personal information and how it's shared.

Looking ahead, the potential of blockchain and cryptocurrencies is enormous. From decentralizing finance (DeFi) and enabling more transparent voting systems, to the creation of decentralized autonomous organizations (DAOs) and even tokenized assets like real estate and art, the possibilities are endless. In the coming years, blockchain technology could reshape entire industries and create new forms of economic value that we can't yet fully imagine.

A Glimpse of the Road Ahead

While blockchain and cryptocurrencies have already demonstrated their disruptive potential, we're still in the early stages of this technological revolution. There are challenges to overcome, such as scalability, regulatory uncertainty, and environmental concerns related to mining, but the momentum is undeniable. As more developers, innovators, and governments work together to refine and improve these technologies, the roadmap ahead looks promising.

One thing is certain: we are on the cusp of a new era. The future of blockchain and cryptocurrencies isn't just about digital money; it's about the democratization of trust and the power to transact, collaborate, and create in entirely new ways. Whether you're a skeptic, a curious observer, or an early adopter, the road ahead is one worth watching—and perhaps even traveling.

In the chapters that follow, we'll dive deeper into these technologies, exploring how they work, what they mean for the future, and how you can get involved. Let's take the first step together.

Chapter 1: The Basics of Blockchain and Cryptocurrencies

1.1 What is Blockchain?

Definition of Blockchain

Blockchain is a revolutionary technology that's often described as a **decentralized ledger** of transactions. To understand it fully, let's break down each of the key characteristics that make it so unique and powerful: decentralization, immutability, transparency, and peer-to-peer security.

A Decentralized Ledger of Transactions

At its core, a blockchain is a distributed digital ledger. A **ledger** is simply a record of transactions—much like the ledger a business might use to track financial accounts. But instead of being stored in a centralized location, such as a bank or a server owned by a single entity, this ledger is **decentralized**, meaning it is distributed across a network of computers (or "nodes") that work together to validate and store transactions.

This decentralized nature means that no single authority (like a bank or government) controls the blockchain. Instead, multiple participants in the network maintain a copy of the ledger. Every time a new transaction is made, it's broadcast to the network, and a consensus must be reached among the nodes before the transaction is added to the ledger. This system removes the need for a trusted intermediary, such as a financial institution, and allows transactions to happen directly between users—hence the term **peer-to-peer**.

In the context of cryptocurrencies, this means that Bitcoin or Ethereum transactions are validated by the network, not by any centralized party. It's this decentralization that enables blockchain to function as a **trustless** system—participants don't have to trust a central authority or middleman because the rules of the system are encoded in the blockchain itself.

Immutable and Transparent Records

One of the most powerful features of blockchain is that it provides **immutable** and **transparent** records. Once a transaction is added to the blockchain, it becomes nearly impossible to change or delete. This is due to the way data is structured on the blockchain.

Each block of data in the blockchain contains a list of transactions, a timestamp, and a cryptographic hash of the previous block. This chain of blocks is linked together in such a way that changing any part of a block would require altering every subsequent block, which is computationally infeasible without taking control of the majority of the network (which, in most large blockchains, would be extremely difficult).

This ensures that once a transaction is recorded, it cannot be tampered with or reversed.

The **immutability** of blockchain makes it a powerful tool for industries where data integrity is crucial, such as finance, healthcare, and supply chain management. For example, in supply chains, once a product's journey has been recorded on the blockchain, that record cannot be altered or falsified, ensuring the authenticity of the product's history.

In addition to immutability, blockchain also offers **transparency**. Every participant in the network can access the entire history of transactions, which are publicly visible (though typically pseudonymous, depending on the blockchain). This transparency promotes trust among users because it ensures that anyone can verify the data at any time, without needing to rely on an intermediary or third party.

Peer-to-Peer Network for Secure Data Sharing

Blockchain operates on a **peer-to-peer (P2P)** network, meaning that data is shared directly between participants without the need for a central server. Each node on the network maintains a copy of the entire blockchain and is responsible for validating transactions.

When a new transaction is initiated, it is broadcast to all participants in the network. The nodes use algorithms to ensure that the transaction is valid (for example, verifying that the sender has sufficient funds to complete the transaction). In systems like Bitcoin, this is achieved through a process called **mining**, where participants compete to solve complex cryptographic puzzles in order to add new blocks to the blockchain. In other systems, different consensus mechanisms like **proof of stake** may be used.

This decentralized, peer-to-peer structure ensures that data is shared in a secure and distributed way. Unlike centralized systems, where a single point of failure can result in a breach or data loss, blockchain's decentralized nature makes it much more resilient. It also means that blockchain can operate in environments where trust is scarce or where traditional intermediaries are not available or desirable.

Furthermore, the data exchanged on the blockchain is **cryptographically secured**, ensuring that transactions are not only verified by the network but also protected against fraud or manipulation. This cryptographic security is what makes blockchain transactions so reliable and tamper-proof.

In Summary

Blockchain is much more than just a new way to handle transactions; it's a transformative technology that offers **decentralized**, **immutable**, and **transparent** records of data. It enables peer-to-peer transactions without the need for intermediaries, and its decentralized ledger ensures that no single entity controls the system. This combination of decentralization, transparency, immutability, and cryptographic security is what makes blockchain such a powerful tool for creating trust in a digital world.

In the chapters that follow, we'll dive deeper into how these core principles of blockchain can be applied across various industries—and how they're changing the way we think about data, money, and trust.

How Blockchain Works

Now that you understand the core concept of blockchain as a decentralized, immutable ledger, let's explore how it actually works behind the scenes. The magic of blockchain is in its structure and the technology that enables it to function securely, efficiently, and autonomously. Key components like **blocks, chains, miners, consensus mechanisms**, and **cryptographic hashing** come together to create a system that is both transparent and secure.

Blocks, Chains, and Miners

At its most basic level, blockchain is made up of **blocks** of data, each containing a record of transactions. These blocks are linked together in a chronological order, forming a **chain**—hence the name "blockchain."

1. **Blocks**: A block is like a page in a ledger, and it holds several key pieces of information:

- **Transaction data**: A record of all the transactions that have occurred during a particular time period. For example, in Bitcoin, each transaction would record details such as the sender's address, the receiver's address, and the amount transferred.
- **Timestamp**: The date and time when the block was added to the blockchain.
- **Previous block hash**: A cryptographic fingerprint that links the current block to the previous block in the chain, creating an unbroken sequence of blocks.

1. **Chains**: When a new block is added to the blockchain, it references the previous block via its **hash**. This creates an unalterable chain, where each block is inherently connected to the one before it. If someone tries to tamper with one block—say, by changing the transaction data or the timestamp—the hash of that block would change, breaking the chain and immediately alerting the network that something is wrong. This makes the blockchain secure and immutable.

2. **Miners**: In some blockchain systems, like Bitcoin, new blocks are added through a process called **mining**. Miners are participants in the network who use computational power to solve complex mathematical puzzles in order to add new blocks to the blockchain. The first miner to solve the puzzle gets the right to add the block and is rewarded with a certain number of cryptocurrency tokens (for Bitcoin, this is a reward of new Bitcoin).

Mining is a competitive process, and it requires a significant amount of computing power, which is why it's often referred to as a **proof of work** mechanism (more on that in a moment). The miner who successfully adds a block is also responsible for verifying the transactions within it, ensuring that they are legitimate before adding them to the blockchain.

Consensus Mechanisms (Proof of Work, Proof of Stake)

One of the key challenges for blockchain networks is how to ensure that all participants agree on the contents of the blockchain, especially when there's no central authority to dictate what is correct. This is where **consensus mechanisms** come in. They are protocols that help participants reach an agreement on which transactions are valid and which blocks should be added to the chain.

There are a number of different consensus mechanisms, but the two most prominent are **Proof of Work (PoW)** and **Proof of Stake (PoS)**.

1. **Proof of Work (PoW)**: This is the consensus mechanism used by Bitcoin and many other blockchains. In PoW, miners compete to solve complex cryptographic puzzles. These puzzles are difficult to solve, but easy to verify once solved. The first miner to solve the puzzle gets the right to add a new block to the blockchain.

- **The Puzzle**: The puzzle is essentially a cryptographic calculation that requires significant computational effort. Miners repeatedly hash data from the block (including the block's previous hash and the current block's data) until they find a hash that meets a predefined criterion, like starting with a certain number of zeros.
- **Security**: This system makes tampering with the blockchain extremely difficult. In order to alter a past block, an attacker would have to redo the work for that block *and every subsequent block*, which would require an enormous amount of computational power. This ensures the integrity of the blockchain.

1. The drawback of PoW is its **energy consumption**. Because miners must solve these complex puzzles, the process requires significant computational power, which results in a large environmental footprint.

2. **Proof of Stake (PoS)**: Proof of Stake is a more energy-efficient alternative to PoW, used by blockchains like Ethereum 2.0. In PoS, instead of miners, there are **validators**. Validators are chosen to create new blocks based on the number of cryptocurrency tokens they "stake" (i.e., lock up as collateral) on the network. The more tokens a validator stakes, the higher the chances they have of being selected to create the next block.

- **Staking and Rewards**: Validators are rewarded with transaction fees (and sometimes newly minted tokens) for successfully validating blocks. If a validator tries to tamper with the blockchain, they risk losing their staked tokens, which incentivizes honesty.
- **Efficiency and Security**: PoS is generally seen as more energy-efficient because it doesn't require the same computational work as PoW. It also allows for faster transactions and better scalability. However, PoS systems must ensure that the network has a sufficient number of validators to maintain security and decentralization.

Each of these consensus mechanisms is designed to ensure that the blockchain remains secure, decentralized, and resistant to tampering.

Cryptographic Hashing and Security

At the heart of blockchain's security is **cryptographic hashing**. A **hash** is a mathematical function that takes an input (like a piece of transaction data) and turns it into a fixed-length string of characters, which appears random. For example, the Bitcoin network uses the **SHA-256** cryptographic hash function.

Why is this important? Let's break it down:

1. **Immutability and Integrity**: When a block is added to the blockchain, the hash of the previous block is included in the new block. This ensures that if anyone tries to alter a block, the hash will change, breaking the chain and alerting everyone in the network that something is wrong. This is what makes blockchain "immutable" or tamper-resistant.

2. **Security**: Cryptographic hashes also ensure that transactions are secure. Each transaction is verified and recorded in such a way that it is nearly impossible for an attacker to alter the data. Even if someone managed to access the blockchain, altering a single transaction would require them to change all subsequent transactions, which would be computationally impractical without control over the majority of the network.

3. **Public and Private Keys**: Blockchain also uses **public-key cryptography** to secure transactions. Each participant in the network has a **public key** (an address that anyone can use to send them cryptocurrency) and a **private key** (a secret code that proves ownership of the cryptocurrency and allows the user to send it). The private key is never shared with the network—only the public key is visible. When a user wants to send cryptocurrency, they "sign" the transaction with their private key, and the network uses the public key to verify that the transaction was legitimate.

In Summary

Blockchain's functionality comes down to a combination of **blocks**, **chains**, **miners**, and **consensus mechanisms**. Each block holds a set of transactions, linked together in a chain, with miners working to validate and add new blocks through consensus mechanisms like Proof of Work and Proof of Stake. Cryptographic hashing ensures the security of the system by making it virtually impossible to alter past transactions.

This intricate design makes blockchain incredibly secure, transparent, and decentralized, allowing it to operate without the need for a central authority. Understanding how these components work together will help you appreciate why blockchain is such a powerful tool—and why it has the potential to disrupt so many industries in the years to come.

Key Characteristics of Blockchain

Blockchain technology is transforming industries by offering a novel approach to handling data, transactions, and trust. The key characteristics that make blockchain so powerful are **decentralization**, **transparency**, **immutability**, and **security through encryption**. Each of these traits plays a crucial role in how blockchain operates and why it has the potential to disrupt everything from finance to supply chain management.

Decentralization and Trustlessness

One of the most defining features of blockchain is its **decentralized** nature. Unlike traditional systems, where a central authority (such as a bank, government, or corporation) oversees and controls data, blockchain is distributed across a network of computers, called **nodes**. Each participant in the blockchain network has a copy of the entire ledger, and no single entity has control over the entire system.

- **Decentralization** eliminates the need for intermediaries, which is a big part of what makes blockchain so revolutionary. In a traditional financial system, for example, a bank acts as the trusted intermediary between two parties conducting a transaction. With blockchain, transactions happen directly between users in a peer-to-peer network, with no need for a third party to validate or approve them.
- **Trustlessness**: Because blockchain is decentralized, it also operates in a trustless environment. In other words, participants don't need to trust any single person or institution. Instead, they trust the underlying technology—specifically, the protocol and consensus mechanisms that govern the blockchain. This system of trust is built into the blockchain itself, which ensures that all transactions are validated and secure without relying on a central authority.

By removing the middleman and allowing participants to interact directly, blockchain creates an ecosystem where trust is not dependent on any single entity. This is particularly valuable in situations where trust is scarce or where intermediaries are inefficient or costly.

Transparency and Immutability

Transparency and **immutability** are two more fundamental characteristics of blockchain that set it apart from traditional systems.

1. **Transparency**: Blockchain is a public ledger, meaning that all transactions recorded on the blockchain are visible to every participant in the network. This level of transparency ensures that anyone can verify and audit the transactions without the need for permission or approval from any centralized authority.

- For example, in the case of Bitcoin, every transaction is visible on the public blockchain, and anyone can check how many Bitcoins are in a particular wallet or trace the history of any given transaction. This openness helps to foster accountability and trust among users because there is a clear, auditable record of all transactions.
- **Permissionless vs. Permissioned Blockchains**: In **permissionless** blockchains (like Bitcoin and Ethereum), anyone can participate and access the transaction history. In **permissioned** blockchains (often used in enterprise solutions), access may be restricted to certain users, but the underlying principle of transparency still applies within the trusted network.

1. **Immutability**: Once data is recorded on a blockchain, it is incredibly difficult—if not impossible—to alter or erase. This is because each new block in the blockchain contains a **cryptographic hash** of the previous block, creating a

secure chain of blocks. If anyone tries to tamper with the data in one block, the hash will change, which would break the chain and immediately alert the network that something is wrong.

- This characteristic is vital for applications where data integrity is crucial, such as financial transactions, medical records, and supply chain tracking. For example, if someone tried to alter the details of a financial transaction on the blockchain, the hash of that block would no longer match the previous block's hash, making the entire blockchain invalid.

- Immutability also means that blockchain can act as a **permanent record**, where historical data remains intact and accessible for verification, but it cannot be erased or altered once recorded.

Together, **transparency** and **immutability** ensure that blockchain transactions are open, auditable, and resistant to manipulation, which builds confidence and trust in the system.

Security Through Encryption

Blockchain's **security** is powered by advanced **cryptography**. Each transaction is encrypted and verified using cryptographic algorithms, which ensures the integrity, confidentiality, and authenticity of the data. Let's explore how encryption contributes to blockchain security:

1. **Public and Private Key Cryptography**:

- Every participant in a blockchain network has a **public key** (like an account number) and a **private key** (like a password). The public key is used to receive transactions, while the private key is used to sign and authorize transactions.
- When a user wants to send cryptocurrency or execute a contract, they sign the transaction with their private key, which proves they have the right to access the funds or data. The network can then verify the transaction using the public key, ensuring that it was authorized by the rightful owner.
- This cryptographic system ensures that only the holder of the private key can initiate transactions, which prevents unauthorized access and fraud.

1. **Hashing and Data Integrity**:

- Blockchain uses **hashing** to secure transactions and ensure data integrity. When a block is created, the transaction data is passed through a cryptographic hashing function (such as SHA-256 in Bitcoin). This generates a unique string of characters (the hash) that represents the data in the block.
- If someone attempts to change the data in a block, the hash will change, which would break the link between that block and the next one. This ensures that the blockchain remains intact and tamper-resistant.
- Each new block contains the hash of the previous block, creating a **chain** of blocks that is incredibly difficult to alter. This method of linking blocks together through hashes is what makes blockchain "immutable."

1. **Consensus Mechanisms and Security**:

- Blockchain networks also use **consensus mechanisms** (such as Proof of Work or Proof of Stake) to secure the system. These mechanisms ensure that participants in the network agree on the state of the blockchain and prevent malicious actors from making unauthorized changes to the ledger.
- In Proof of Work (PoW), miners must solve complex mathematical problems to add new blocks, and they are incentivized to act honestly because they risk losing their stake if they attempt to manipulate the system.
- In Proof of Stake (PoS), validators are selected to create new blocks based on the number of tokens they have staked, and they are incentivized to act honestly by the threat of losing their staked tokens if they validate fraudulent transactions.

These layers of cryptographic security, from public and private keys to consensus protocols, make blockchain a highly secure technology, resistant to hacking, fraud, and manipulation.

In Summary

The key characteristics of blockchain—**decentralization, trustlessness, transparency, immutability**, and **security through encryption**—work together to create a system that is open, secure, and resistant to fraud. By eliminating intermediaries and central authorities, blockchain enables trustless transactions and opens up new possibilities for decentralized applications across a wide range of industries.

- **Decentralization** removes the need for a trusted third party and ensures that control is distributed across the network.
- **Transparency** allows for greater accountability and auditability, ensuring that anyone can verify transactions.
- **Immutability** ensures that once data is added to the blockchain, it cannot be altered or erased, protecting the integrity of the system.
- **Security through encryption** guarantees that data is secure, authenticated, and resistant to tampering, making blockchain a highly reliable technology for handling sensitive information.

These characteristics are what make blockchain so transformative and capable of disrupting everything from finance to healthcare, supply chain management, and beyond. Understanding them is the first step in appreciating the full potential of blockchain technology.

1.2 What is Cryptocurrency?

Defining Cryptocurrency

Cryptocurrency is a **digital** or **virtual currency** that uses **cryptography** for secure financial transactions, controls the creation of new units, and verifies the transfer of assets. Unlike traditional currencies issued by governments (fiat currencies), cryptocurrencies operate on decentralized networks, primarily using **blockchain** technology to enable secure and transparent transactions. This means that cryptocurrency transactions are not controlled by any central authority, such as a bank or government, but rather by a network of nodes (computers) that participate in the validation of transactions.

Digital or Virtual Currency Using Cryptography

Cryptocurrency exists entirely in digital form, which means it has no physical counterpart like coins or paper money. Instead, it is a digital asset that can be transferred, stored, and traded electronically. Cryptocurrencies rely on **cryptographic techniques** to secure transactions, control the creation of new units, and verify the transfer of assets between users. These cryptographic techniques ensure the **integrity** and **security** of cryptocurrency networks.

One of the primary advantages of using cryptography in cryptocurrency is its ability to prevent fraud and double-spending, as well as ensure that transactions are irreversible once confirmed. Cryptographic algorithms, such as **SHA-256** in Bitcoin or **Ethash** in Ethereum, are used to secure the transaction data, which is then recorded on the blockchain.

Operates on a Decentralized Network (Blockchain)

Cryptocurrencies run on decentralized networks, meaning no central authority governs or controls them. Instead of being issued or managed by a central institution like a bank or government, cryptocurrency transactions are validated by **a distributed network of computers** (or **nodes**). These nodes communicate and work together to maintain the **blockchain**, a public ledger that records all transactions.

In the case of Bitcoin, for example, miners on the network use computational power to validate transactions and secure the blockchain. In other cryptocurrencies, such as **Ethereum**, a different consensus mechanism (Proof of Stake) may be used, but the core concept remains the same: decentralization, which eliminates the need for trusted third parties.

This decentralization provides several key benefits:

- **Security**: Because the blockchain is distributed across thousands or even millions of computers, it is difficult to hack or manipulate.
- **Censorship-resistance**: No central authority can freeze, seize, or restrict access to cryptocurrency accounts or transactions.
- **Transparency**: Anyone can view the transaction history of any cryptocurrency in the network, promoting transparency and accountability.

Examples: Bitcoin, Ethereum, and Altcoins

The most well-known cryptocurrency is **Bitcoin**, which was created in 2009 by an anonymous entity known as **Satoshi Nakamoto**. Bitcoin remains the first and largest cryptocurrency by market capitalization, and it is primarily used as a store of value and a means of transferring funds across borders without the need for intermediaries.

Following Bitcoin's success, **Ethereum** was introduced in 2015 by **Vitalik Buterin** and others. Ethereum is unique in that it not only functions as a cryptocurrency (Ether or ETH) but also provides a decentralized platform for building **smart contracts** and **decentralized applications (dApps)**. These capabilities have allowed Ethereum to become a foundational layer for many other decentralized projects in the blockchain space.

In addition to Bitcoin and Ethereum, there are thousands of other cryptocurrencies, known as **altcoins** (short for "alternative coins"). Some popular examples of altcoins include:

- **Litecoin (LTC)**: Often referred to as the "silver" to Bitcoin's "gold," Litecoin is a peer-to-peer cryptocurrency that aims to be faster and more efficient than Bitcoin.
- **Ripple (XRP)**: Focuses on providing fast, low-cost cross-border payments for financial institutions.
- **Cardano (ADA)**: A blockchain platform for building smart contracts and dApps, similar to Ethereum, but with a focus on sustainability and scalability.

Each of these cryptocurrencies operates on a decentralized network and uses cryptographic principles, but they may differ in their specific goals, technologies, and use cases.

In Summary

Cryptocurrency is a **digital currency** that uses **cryptography** to secure transactions and operate on a **decentralized blockchain network**. By eliminating intermediaries and central authorities, cryptocurrencies offer users greater control over their own assets and allow for fast, secure, and transparent transactions. Bitcoin, Ethereum, and altcoins represent the diverse ecosystem of cryptocurrencies that are continually evolving to meet different use cases and solve real-world problems.

How Cryptocurrencies Work

Understanding how cryptocurrencies work is essential to appreciating their value and functionality in the digital economy. At the heart of cryptocurrency transactions are several key components, including **wallets**, the **transaction process**, **mining** vs. **staking**, and the role of **public and private keys**. Let's break down each of these components to see how they contribute to the seamless operation of cryptocurrencies.

Transaction Process and Wallets

The transaction process in a cryptocurrency network involves the transfer of digital assets (like Bitcoin or Ethereum) from one user to another. This process is initiated through a **cryptocurrency wallet**—a software application that allows users to store, send, and receive cryptocurrency.

- **Wallets**: A cryptocurrency wallet consists of two main parts: a **public key** and a **private key** (more on this below). The wallet's public key is like an account number that can be shared with others to receive funds, while the private key is like a password that must be kept secure to access and send funds. A wallet can be:
- **Hot Wallet**: A software-based wallet connected to the internet, suitable for frequent transactions but more vulnerable to hacks.
- **Cold Wallet**: A hardware or paper wallet that is not connected to the internet, offering enhanced security but less convenient for regular transactions.

When a user wants to send cryptocurrency to another user, they generate a **transaction request** within their wallet, which includes:

- The amount to send
- The recipient's **public address** (wallet address)
- A **digital signature**, created by the sender using their private key, to verify the authenticity of the transaction.

Once the transaction is broadcast to the network, it gets validated and added to the **blockchain** through the mining or staking process.

Mining vs. Staking

The **mining** and **staking** processes are used to secure the cryptocurrency network and validate transactions, but they operate differently depending on the consensus mechanism used by the network.

1. **Mining (Proof of Work):**

- Mining is the process used by Bitcoin and many other cryptocurrencies that rely on **Proof of Work** (PoW). In PoW, miners use powerful computers to solve complex mathematical puzzles, which require significant computational resources.
- When a miner successfully solves a puzzle, they **validate** the transactions within a block and add it to the blockchain. In return for their efforts, miners are rewarded with cryptocurrency (e.g., new Bitcoin).

- This process ensures that the blockchain remains secure and that no one can easily alter transaction history. It also makes it costly for malicious actors to attack the network, as altering past blocks would require an immense amount of computational power.

1. **Staking (Proof of Stake)**:

- Staking is used by cryptocurrencies like **Ethereum 2.0** and **Cardano** that operate on a **Proof of Stake** (PoS) consensus mechanism. In PoS, participants (called **validators**) lock up or "stake" a certain amount of cryptocurrency in the network as collateral.
- Instead of solving computational puzzles like miners, validators are selected to create new blocks and validate transactions based on the amount of cryptocurrency they have staked and other factors, like how long they've held their stake.
- The advantage of staking is that it consumes far less energy than mining and can offer faster transaction processing times. Validators are rewarded with transaction fees and possibly new cryptocurrency tokens for their efforts. If they act dishonestly, they risk losing their staked funds.

The Role of Public and Private Keys

The **public key** and **private key** form the backbone of cryptocurrency transactions. These cryptographic keys ensure that the ownership and transfer of digital assets are secure and verifiable.

1. **Public Key**:

- The public key is like an **account number** that others can use to send you cryptocurrency. It is freely shared and acts as an address to receive funds.
- Anyone who has your public key can send cryptocurrency to your wallet. However, the public key alone cannot be used to access or transfer funds.

1. **Private Key**:

- The private key is like a **password** or **PIN code** that is **unique** to you and should be kept secure at all costs. It is used to **sign** transactions and prove ownership of the cryptocurrency in your wallet.
- When you initiate a transaction, you use your private key to digitally sign it, creating a **digital signature** that authenticates the transaction and authorizes the transfer of funds from your wallet.
- If someone gains access to your private key, they can send your cryptocurrency to their own wallet, which is why it is critical to keep this key secure (preferably offline in a **cold wallet**).

Together, the **public** and **private keys** enable secure, peer-to-peer transactions without needing a third party like a bank or payment processor. The combination of these keys ensures that only the legitimate owner of the cryptocurrency can authorize its transfer.

In Summary

Cryptocurrencies work by using digital wallets and cryptographic keys to enable secure, decentralized transactions. Here's a quick breakdown of the key components:

- **Transaction Process and Wallets**: Users store their cryptocurrency in wallets, which contain a **public key** for receiving funds and a **private key** for signing transactions and accessing funds.
- **Mining vs. Staking**:
- **Mining (PoW)** uses computational power to validate transactions and add blocks to the blockchain.
- **Staking (PoS)** involves locking up cryptocurrency as collateral to validate transactions with far less energy consumption.
- **Public and Private Keys**: Public keys act as an address to receive cryptocurrency, while private keys are used to authorize transactions and prove ownership.

Why Cryptocurrencies Matter

Cryptocurrencies are not just a technological innovation; they represent a profound shift in the way we think about and interact with money. They have the potential to **disrupt traditional financial systems, empower individuals**, and offer **financial inclusion** to populations that have been historically underserved by traditional banking systems. Let's dive into these key points and explore why cryptocurrencies matter in today's world.

Disruption of Traditional Financial Systems

For centuries, the global financial system has been built on centralized institutions such as banks, governments, and other intermediaries. These institutions control the flow of money, enforce monetary policy, and act as gatekeepers for transactions. While this system has worked in many ways, it has also created inefficiencies, high costs, and centralized control that can limit access to financial services.

Cryptocurrencies, powered by **blockchain technology**, offer a **decentralized alternative** to these traditional systems. By removing intermediaries and allowing for direct, peer-to-peer transactions, cryptocurrencies eliminate the need for banks or payment processors to facilitate transfers, reducing transaction fees, delays, and administrative overhead.

Some of the key ways cryptocurrencies disrupt traditional finance include:

- **Global Accessibility**: Cryptocurrencies can be accessed by anyone with an internet connection, regardless of their location, background, or financial status.
- **Lower Transaction Costs**: By cutting out intermediaries, cryptocurrencies can enable faster and cheaper cross-border transactions.
- **Censorship Resistance**: In some countries, cryptocurrencies provide a way to circumvent government censorship and control over citizens' finances, enabling individuals to transact freely.

As these technologies continue to evolve, cryptocurrencies could challenge the dominance of traditional financial systems and lead to the emergence of more decentralized and efficient financial services.

Empowering Individuals and Reducing Intermediaries

One of the most exciting aspects of cryptocurrency is how it empowers **individuals** by giving them more control over their financial activities. In traditional finance, users rely on banks, credit card companies, and other financial institutions to conduct transactions, manage accounts, and provide services. These intermediaries often impose fees, delay transactions, and limit access to financial products based on location, credit score, or other factors.

Cryptocurrencies shift the balance of power by enabling **peer-to-peer transactions**. This means that users can send and receive money directly, without the need for banks or payment processors. Key benefits of this empowerment include:

- **Financial Control**: Users have full ownership and control over their assets without relying on third parties.
- **Privacy**: Many cryptocurrencies (like Bitcoin or Monero) offer greater privacy than traditional payment systems, giving users more control over their financial data.
- **Autonomy**: Cryptocurrencies allow individuals to take part in global markets, invest in digital assets, and access decentralized financial services, all on their own terms.

This democratization of financial access is particularly important for individuals in regions where traditional banking infrastructure is lacking or where people face systemic barriers to financial services.

Financial Inclusion for Unbanked Populations

Around the world, **billions of people** remain unbanked or underbanked, meaning they have little or no access to traditional banking services like savings accounts, loans, or credit. The reasons for this are varied: geographic isolation, poverty, lack of identification, or simply the high costs and barriers to entry in traditional banking systems.

Cryptocurrencies can change this by providing a low-cost, decentralized alternative to traditional financial services. All that is needed to access a cryptocurrency network is an **internet connection** and a **smartphone**. Here's how cryptocurrencies contribute to **financial inclusion**:

- **No Need for a Bank Account**: Cryptocurrencies allow individuals to store and transfer value without the need for a bank account or physical infrastructure.
- **Microtransactions**: Cryptocurrencies can enable very small payments (often called **microtransactions**), which is especially useful in developing economies where traditional financial systems struggle to serve small-scale transactions.
- **Access to Global Markets**: By using cryptocurrency, people in underserved regions can access the global economy, participate in e-commerce, or invest in digital assets like cryptocurrencies or tokenized assets.

For people in rural or remote areas, cryptocurrencies can offer an easy and affordable way to access financial services and connect with the global economy without relying on traditional banking institutions.

In Summary

Cryptocurrencies matter because they:

- **Disrupt traditional financial systems** by enabling decentralized, peer-to-peer transactions that bypass intermediaries like banks and payment processors.
- **Empower individuals** by giving them more control over their financial activities, reducing reliance on centralized authorities, and providing greater privacy and autonomy.
- Offer **financial inclusion** to **unbanked populations** by enabling access to digital financial services with nothing more than an internet connection and a smartphone.

The potential for cryptocurrencies to reshape the financial landscape is immense, particularly as technology improves and adoption grows. By addressing some of the most pressing issues with traditional finance—costs, inefficiency, and lack of access—cryptocurrencies offer a new vision for the future of money.

1.3 How Blockchain and Cryptocurrencies Are Connected

Blockchain as the Backbone of Cryptocurrency

Blockchain is the technology that underpins and powers most cryptocurrencies. It provides the **secure, decentralized infrastructure** necessary for cryptocurrency transactions to be valid, transparent, and trustworthy. By using blockchain, cryptocurrencies are able to achieve features like **decentralization**, **security**, and **immutability**—all without the need for centralized intermediaries like banks or payment processors. Let's explore how blockchain functions as the backbone of cryptocurrency, focusing on its role in enabling secure transactions, facilitating decentralization, and the specific relationship between **Bitcoin** and its blockchain.

Blockchain's Role in Enabling Secure Transactions

One of the core reasons cryptocurrencies work securely and effectively is because of blockchain's inherent design. Blockchain is a **distributed ledger** that records all transactions across a network of computers (called **nodes**). Each transaction is encrypted and bundled into a **block**, and these blocks are then linked together to form an immutable chain.

Key characteristics that make blockchain secure include:

- **Immutability**: Once data is added to a blockchain, it cannot be altered or deleted. This ensures the integrity of the transaction history.
- **Decentralization**: Blockchain operates on a **peer-to-peer network**, meaning no single entity controls the network. This eliminates single points of failure and reduces the risk of fraud or tampering.

- **Cryptographic Security**: Transactions on the blockchain are verified using cryptographic techniques. Each transaction is encrypted, and each block is linked to the previous one via a **hash**, making it extremely difficult to alter past transaction records.

By using blockchain, cryptocurrencies can offer a level of **security** and **trust** that is not reliant on any single party. This makes it particularly suitable for **financial transactions**, as users can trust the system to prevent fraud, double-spending, and tampering.

How Cryptocurrencies Use Blockchain to Achieve Decentralization

Blockchain is what enables cryptocurrencies to be **decentralized**. In traditional financial systems, a central authority (like a bank or government) manages and verifies transactions. However, in a blockchain-based cryptocurrency system, no central authority is needed. Instead, the network of nodes collectively validates and records transactions on the blockchain. Here's how blockchain enables decentralization:

- **Distributed Ledger**: Blockchain's distributed nature means that all participants (nodes) in the network have a copy of the entire transaction history. This eliminates the need for centralized record-keeping, as everyone on the network can verify transactions independently.
- **Consensus Mechanism**: In order for a new block to be added to the blockchain, the majority of the network participants must agree that the transactions in that block

are valid. This is done through a **consensus mechanism**, such as **Proof of Work (PoW)** or **Proof of Stake (PoS)**.

- **No Central Authority**: Since no central authority controls the blockchain, cryptocurrencies like Bitcoin are free from the influence or control of governments, banks, or corporations. This is one of the key features of **trustlessness**—trust is placed in the code and the network rather than in a third-party intermediary.

The decentralized nature of blockchain technology ensures that cryptocurrencies can operate in a **peer-to-peer** manner, without the need for intermediaries, and without the risk of a central authority's interference or failure.

The Relationship Between Bitcoin and Its Blockchain

Bitcoin was the first cryptocurrency to use blockchain technology, and the two are deeply intertwined. Bitcoin's blockchain is a **public ledger** that records every transaction made using Bitcoin, and it plays a crucial role in maintaining the security and integrity of the Bitcoin network. Here's how Bitcoin and its blockchain work together:

- **Bitcoin as a Digital Asset**: Bitcoin itself is a **digital asset** that represents value. It can be transferred between users, bought, sold, or stored in a digital wallet.
- **Bitcoin Blockchain**: The Bitcoin blockchain is the technology that enables these transactions. Every time someone sends Bitcoin, the transaction is broadcast to the Bitcoin network and added to the blockchain after being validated by miners using the **Proof of Work (PoW)**

consensus mechanism.

- **Mining and Block Rewards**: Miners use their computational power to solve complex mathematical puzzles and validate transactions. Once a puzzle is solved, the miner adds the new block of transactions to the Bitcoin blockchain and is rewarded with newly minted Bitcoin and transaction fees. This incentivizes miners to maintain the security and integrity of the blockchain.

The Bitcoin blockchain is **immutable**, meaning once a transaction is recorded, it is permanent and cannot be changed. This ensures that the history of Bitcoin transactions remains transparent, auditable, and secure.

In Summary

Blockchain is the foundational technology behind cryptocurrencies, providing the structure needed to securely validate transactions and achieve **decentralization**. It enables cryptocurrencies to:

- **Ensure secure transactions** through cryptographic encryption and an immutable ledger.
- **Achieve decentralization** by removing intermediaries and enabling peer-to-peer transaction validation via a distributed network.
- **Maintain the relationship between Bitcoin and its blockchain**, where the blockchain serves as the public ledger for Bitcoin transactions, enabling its use as a secure and trusted digital currency.

Why Blockchain is More than Just Crypto

While blockchain is best known for its use in powering cryptocurrencies like Bitcoin and Ethereum, its potential goes far beyond just digital currency. Blockchain technology has the ability to **revolutionize various industries** by providing secure, transparent, and efficient systems for managing data, verifying transactions, and automating processes. This section will explore the **diverse applications** of blockchain beyond cryptocurrency, highlighting **smart contracts**, **supply chain management**, and other industry-transforming use cases.

Blockchain's Use Beyond Currency

Blockchain is essentially a **decentralized, immutable ledger** that can be used to track and record data in a transparent and secure way. This technology has a wide range of applications beyond digital currencies, including:

1. **Smart Contracts**:

- Smart contracts are self-executing contracts with the terms of the agreement directly written into lines of code. They automatically execute actions (such as payments or asset transfers) when predefined conditions are met.
- For example, a smart contract could automatically transfer ownership of a property when a payment is received, or release funds from an escrow account once both parties meet the agreed-upon terms. This reduces the need for

intermediaries like lawyers or banks and can increase efficiency, transparency, and security.

1. **Supply Chain Management**:

- Blockchain can be used to **track the journey of products** from the source to the consumer, ensuring the integrity of data along the way. Every step in the supply chain, from raw materials to final delivery, can be recorded on a blockchain.
- This enables **greater transparency**, **reduced fraud**, and better accountability. For instance, consumers can trace the origin of their food or clothing and verify its ethical sourcing.
- **Supply chain applications** in industries like agriculture, pharmaceuticals, and manufacturing can improve tracking, reduce counterfeiting, and optimize inventory management.

1. **Healthcare**:

- Blockchain can securely store and share patient records, ensuring that data is accurate and accessible to authorized parties only. It can also streamline the process of managing medical billing and insurance claims.
- Healthcare providers can use blockchain to create **decentralized patient records**, enabling patients to control their own health data and share it easily across various healthcare providers.

1. **Voting Systems**:

41

- Blockchain can create **secure, transparent, and tamper-proof voting systems**. By recording votes on a blockchain, the election process can be more transparent, preventing fraud and ensuring that results are accurate and verifiable.
- This can help increase public trust in electoral systems and provide a more efficient and cost-effective way to conduct elections.

1. **Intellectual Property and Copyright**:

- Blockchain technology can be used to track ownership and usage of digital intellectual property. For example, artists, musicians, and writers can register their works on the blockchain, providing proof of ownership and a transparent record of royalties and usage.
- This can help prevent piracy, ensure creators are fairly compensated, and reduce disputes over intellectual property rights.

Examples of Non-Cryptocurrency Blockchain Applications

Beyond the core use case of cryptocurrencies, many industries are exploring how blockchain can improve their operations and services. Here are a few examples of how blockchain is being used outside the realm of cryptocurrency:

1. **Real Estate**:

- Blockchain can simplify property transactions by elimi-

nating the need for intermediaries, reducing fraud, and ensuring the security and authenticity of property titles.
- By recording property ownership and transactions on the blockchain, buyers and sellers can have confidence in the accuracy of property titles and avoid costly paperwork and legal disputes.

1. **Energy and Utilities**:

- Blockchain can help **decentralize energy markets** by enabling peer-to-peer energy trading. For example, solar energy users can sell excess energy directly to other consumers through blockchain-based platforms, reducing reliance on central power grids and intermediaries.
- It can also be used to track the provenance of energy sources, helping consumers make informed choices about the environmental impact of their energy consumption.

1. **Insurance**:

- Blockchain can streamline the **insurance claims process** by creating smart contracts that automatically process claims when predefined conditions are met, reducing paperwork, administrative costs, and the risk of fraud.
- Additionally, blockchain can help create more transparent and efficient **peer-to-peer insurance** models, where individuals can pool their resources and self-insure with a decentralized, trusted platform.

1. **Digital Identity**:

- Blockchain can provide a **secure, verifiable identity system** that allows individuals to control their personal data. Instead of relying on centralized identity providers (such as governments or corporations), individuals can use blockchain to manage and share their identity securely.
- This has significant implications for **online privacy**, enabling individuals to prove their identity without exposing unnecessary personal information or relying on third parties.

The Potential of Blockchain to Transform Industries

Blockchain's ability to offer **secure, transparent, and decentralized solutions** gives it the potential to transform a wide range of industries. In addition to the applications already discussed, blockchain can enhance:

- **Financial Services**: Blockchain can make payments faster, cheaper, and more secure, enabling cross-border transactions without the need for traditional banking intermediaries.
- **Supply Chain**: Improved tracking of goods, reduced fraud, and more efficient processes across the entire supply chain.
- **Legal and Compliance**: Automating contracts, reducing legal disputes, and ensuring that all parties involved are in agreement and comply with the rules.
- **Education**: Providing verifiable and tamper-proof records of educational achievements and certifications.

As more industries experiment with blockchain, its potential to **disrupt** and **improve** traditional systems becomes increasingly clear. It is not just the future of cryptocurrency; it is a powerful tool that can drive innovation and create more efficient, transparent, and secure systems across multiple sectors.

Cryptocurrency as an Application of Blockchain Technology

Cryptocurrency is one of the most prominent and successful use cases for blockchain technology, and its popularity has driven interest in both the underlying technology and its potential applications. Cryptocurrencies leverage blockchain's decentralized, secure, and transparent features to create a new form of **digital currency** that operates outside the control of traditional financial systems. Let's explore how cryptocurrencies are a direct application of blockchain technology, focusing on **tokenization**, **digital assets**, and how cryptocurrencies are reshaping the **landscape of payments**.

Cryptocurrencies as a Use Case for Blockchain

At its core, cryptocurrency is a **digital or virtual currency** that uses cryptographic principles to secure transactions and control the creation of new units. Blockchain provides the perfect infrastructure for cryptocurrencies by offering a **decentralized ledger** that ensures transparency, immutability, and security.

Cryptocurrencies like **Bitcoin**, **Ethereum**, and others rely on blockchain's distributed network of nodes to verify and record transactions without needing a centralized authority. Each transaction is validated by participants in the network (using mechanisms like **Proof of Work** or **Proof of Stake**) and recorded in blocks on the blockchain, creating a **public, transparent record** of all transactions.

Because blockchain allows for **peer-to-peer transactions**, cryptocurrencies enable users to send money directly to one another without relying on banks, payment processors, or other intermediaries. This decentralization is one of the primary reasons cryptocurrencies have gained popularity, offering an alternative to traditional financial systems.

The Concept of Tokenization and Digital Assets

In the world of cryptocurrency, the concept of **tokenization** is key to understanding how digital assets are created, traded, and managed. Tokenization is the process of converting real-world assets (such as real estate, art, or stocks) or digital representations (such as coins or tokens) into a form that can be traded on a blockchain.

1. **Tokens as Digital Assets**: Cryptocurrencies themselves are **tokens**—digital representations of value that can be used to buy, sell, or trade goods and services. Bitcoin (BTC), for example, is a digital token that represents a unit of value within its blockchain ecosystem.
2. **Non-Fungible Tokens (NFTs)**: A specialized form of tokenization is seen in **Non-Fungible Tokens (NFTs)**, which represent unique digital assets such as art, music, or collectibles. Unlike cryptocurrencies (which are fungible),

NFTs are one-of-a-kind, providing a way to digitally prove ownership and provenance of unique items.

3. **Tokenized Real-World Assets**: Blockchain can also be used to tokenize **real-world assets** like real estate or gold, allowing ownership to be transferred digitally. This opens up new opportunities for fractional ownership, where people can own parts of expensive assets, making previously inaccessible investments more inclusive.

Tokenization allows for **increased liquidity** and **fractional ownership** of assets, democratizing access to investment opportunities and making it easier to buy, sell, and trade assets across different blockchain platforms.

How Cryptocurrencies Are Changing the Landscape of Payments

Cryptocurrencies are transforming the world of payments by offering **faster**, **cheaper**, and more **secure** alternatives to traditional payment methods. Here's how cryptocurrencies are changing the payments landscape:

1. **Cross-Border Payments**: Traditional international money transfers involve intermediaries such as banks, which can be slow and expensive, especially for cross-border transactions. Cryptocurrencies, however, enable **direct peer-to-peer transfers** across borders without the need for third-party intermediaries. This makes international payments faster, cheaper, and more

efficient.

2. **Reduced Transaction Fees**: Traditional payment systems (like credit cards, PayPal, or bank transfers) charge fees for processing transactions. Cryptocurrencies often offer **lower transaction fees** because there are no intermediaries taking a cut. This is especially beneficial for small payments or micropayments.

3. **Financial Inclusion**: Cryptocurrencies provide a way for people without access to traditional banking infrastructure (the **unbanked**) to participate in the global economy. By using only an **internet connection** and a **digital wallet**, individuals in remote or underserved areas can send and receive payments globally, without relying on a bank or financial institution.

4. **Increased Security**: Cryptocurrencies are secured by **cryptographic algorithms**, making them resistant to fraud and identity theft. Transactions are verified and recorded on the blockchain, ensuring a **transparent**, **tamper-proof** record of payments.

5. **Smart Payments**: Many cryptocurrencies, especially those built on the Ethereum blockchain, allow for the use of **smart contracts**. These are self-executing contracts where the terms of an agreement are directly written into code and automatically executed once the predefined conditions are met. This can make payments more **efficient**, **automated**, and **secure**.

In summary, cryptocurrencies are fundamentally changing how we think about **value transfer** and **payments**. They are reducing the friction involved in traditional payment systems, offering new solutions for cross-border transactions, and increasing **financial access** globally.

Chapter 2: How Blockchain and Cryptocurrency Work in Practice

2.1 The Technology Behind Blockchain

Decentralized Networks and Peer-to-Peer Systems

One of the key features of blockchain technology is its **decentralized nature**. Instead of relying on a central authority to control or verify transactions, blockchain networks distribute this responsibility across a **peer-to-peer** (P2P) network of **nodes** (computers or devices). These decentralized networks allow participants to communicate directly with one another, enabling trustless transactions, secure data exchanges, and the elimination of middlemen like banks or payment processors. Let's explore how **nodes** communicate within a blockchain network, why **consensus mechanisms** are crucial for maintaining trust, and how decentralized networks reduce our reliance on centralized authorities.

How Nodes Communicate in a Blockchain Network

In a blockchain network, **nodes** are individual computers that participate in maintaining the decentralized ledger. These nodes are interconnected and share a common protocol, allowing them to communicate and verify transactions without the need for a central entity. Here's how nodes communicate within the network:

1. **Transaction Broadcasting**: When a user initiates a transaction (for example, sending cryptocurrency from one wallet to another), the transaction is broadcast to the network of nodes. Each node receives a copy of the transaction and attempts to validate it.

2. **Validation and Verification**: Nodes validate transactions by checking the **cryptographic signatures** and ensuring that the transaction follows the protocol rules. In a blockchain network, this validation process often involves solving complex cryptographic puzzles or checking the integrity of previous blocks of data. Once validated, the transaction is added to a **block**.

3. **Block Propagation**: Once a node successfully validates a transaction and creates a new block, it propagates the block to other nodes in the network. Each node updates its own copy of the blockchain, ensuring that all participants have a consistent view of the ledger.

4. **Peer-to-Peer Communication**: Nodes communicate with each other in a decentralized, **peer-to-peer** manner, meaning no single node has complete control over the network. This allows blockchain networks to remain resistant to failure, censorship, or manipulation, as there

51

is no central point of attack.

The Importance of Consensus in Maintaining Trust

In a decentralized blockchain network, **consensus** refers to the mechanism by which the nodes agree on the validity of transactions and the order in which they are recorded. Consensus is crucial because, without it, there would be no way to ensure that all participants in the network have the same copy of the ledger and that no fraudulent transactions are added.

Different blockchain networks use various **consensus mechanisms** to achieve agreement. Two of the most common are **Proof of Work (PoW)** and **Proof of Stake (PoS)**:

1. **Proof of Work (PoW)**: In PoW, nodes (called **miners**) compete to solve complex cryptographic puzzles. The first miner to solve the puzzle gets to add the new block to the blockchain and is rewarded with cryptocurrency (e.g., Bitcoin). This process ensures that the majority of nodes agree on the state of the blockchain and that the system is secure against fraud.

2. **Proof of Stake (PoS)**: In PoS, nodes (called **validators**) are selected to create a new block based on the amount of cryptocurrency they "stake" (or lock up as collateral). Validators are incentivized to act honestly because they risk losing their staked coins if they attempt to cheat the system. PoS is considered more energy-efficient than PoW.

The consensus process ensures that **all participants in the**

blockchain agree on the state of the ledger, which helps to maintain **trust** in a decentralized network without the need for a central authority.

Reducing Reliance on Centralized Authorities (e.g., Banks)

One of the most powerful aspects of decentralized blockchain networks is their ability to **reduce or eliminate reliance on centralized authorities** such as banks, governments, and other intermediaries. Traditional financial systems are heavily reliant on centralized institutions to validate transactions, enforce contracts, and maintain trust between parties. Blockchain technology changes this dynamic in several ways:

1. **Peer-to-Peer Transactions**: Blockchain allows for **direct peer-to-peer transactions**, where users can send cryptocurrency or assets to each other without going through a bank or payment processor. This **reduces fees** and **removes intermediaries** from the process, making transactions faster and more cost-effective.

2. **Decentralized Finance (DeFi)**: The rise of **DeFi** applications built on blockchain allows users to access financial services—such as lending, borrowing, and trading—without relying on traditional banks or financial institutions. Smart contracts on blockchain platforms like Ethereum enable these services to be executed autonomously, without human intervention.

3. **Trust Without a Third Party**: In traditional systems, trust is placed in a third party (such as a bank) to verify and authenticate transactions. In blockchain, trust is

distributed across the network, and participants rely on cryptographic validation and consensus mechanisms to ensure the integrity of transactions.

4. **Censorship Resistance**: A decentralized blockchain network is more **resistant to censorship** or control by any single authority. This makes blockchain particularly useful in regions where financial systems are heavily regulated or in situations where individuals want to transact or store value without fear of government oversight or restriction.

By removing the need for centralized intermediaries, blockchain empowers individuals and businesses to operate in a more **autonomous** and **transparent** manner, fostering greater financial inclusion and freedom.

Consensus Mechanisms Explained

One of the core components of blockchain technology is the **consensus mechanism** — the process by which a decentralized network of nodes (computers) agrees on the validity of transactions and the order in which they are recorded on the blockchain. Consensus mechanisms are essential for ensuring that all participants in the network trust the system, and that no single entity can manipulate the blockchain. In this section, we will dive into the most common consensus mechanisms used in blockchain today: **Proof of Work (PoW)** and **Proof of Stake (PoS)**, as well as explore **alternative consensus mechanisms** such as **Delegated Proof of Stake (DPoS)** and **Practical Byzantine Fault Tolerance (PBFT)**.

Proof of Work (PoW) and Its Environmental Impact

Proof of Work (PoW) is the original consensus mechanism used by Bitcoin and many other cryptocurrencies. It is a method where participants (miners) must solve complex cryptographic puzzles in order to validate and add new blocks to the blockchain. The first miner to solve the puzzle gets to add the block and is rewarded with newly minted cryptocurrency (such as Bitcoin).

1. **How PoW Works**:

- Miners compete to solve a cryptographic problem using computational power.
- Once a solution is found, the miner broadcasts the solution to the network, and the other nodes verify the correctness of the solution.
- If the solution is correct, the new block is added to the blockchain, and the miner is rewarded with cryptocurrency.

1. **Environmental Impact of PoW**:

- **Energy Consumption**: PoW requires an enormous amount of computational power, which translates to high energy consumption. Mining Bitcoin, for example, has been criticized for its environmental impact due to the vast amounts of electricity used by miners operating energy-hungry hardware (ASICs).

55

- **Carbon Footprint**: Many Bitcoin miners rely on **non-renewable** energy sources, leading to a significant carbon footprint. Although some miners are transitioning to renewable energy, the overall energy use remains a concern.

While PoW is considered secure and effective for achieving consensus, its **energy inefficiency** has led to growing calls for more sustainable alternatives.

Proof of Stake (PoS) and Energy Efficiency

Proof of Stake (PoS) is an alternative to PoW and has gained significant popularity due to its **energy efficiency** and lower environmental impact. In PoS, validators (instead of miners) participate in the consensus process by staking their cryptocurrency as collateral to propose and validate new blocks.

1. **How PoS Works**:

- Validators must lock up a certain amount of cryptocurrency (their "stake") as collateral in order to participate in the validation process.
- The network selects validators to create new blocks based on the amount of cryptocurrency they have staked and the length of time they have been holding it.
- Validators are rewarded for creating valid blocks and can lose their stake if they attempt to validate fraudulent transactions.

1. **Energy Efficiency**:

- Unlike PoW, PoS does not require massive computational power, which means it consumes far less energy.
- Since validators are chosen based on the amount of cryptocurrency they hold and are incentivized to act honestly, PoS is a much more **environmentally friendly** alternative to PoW.

By **reducing energy consumption** and **incentivizing honest behavior** without the need for mining hardware, PoS offers a more sustainable way to achieve consensus and maintain the integrity of a blockchain.

Alternative Consensus Mechanisms

While PoW and PoS are the most well-known consensus mechanisms, there are other alternatives that aim to solve the issues of scalability, security, and energy efficiency. Two popular alternative consensus mechanisms are **Delegated Proof of Stake (DPoS)** and **Practical Byzantine Fault Tolerance (PBFT)**.

1. **Delegated Proof of Stake (DPoS)**:

- **How DPoS Works**: In DPoS, token holders vote for a smaller group of trusted delegates (also called **witnesses** or **validators**) to validate transactions and create new blocks. This significantly reduces the number of nodes that need to participate in the consensus process, making the network more **efficient** and **scalable**.
- **Efficiency and Speed**: DPoS can process transactions faster than PoW or PoS because only a small group of

validators is responsible for consensus. This makes DPoS ideal for high-transaction platforms and applications that require fast confirmation times.

- **Democratic Element**: DPoS is more **democratic** in that token holders can vote on who gets to be a delegate, giving them more influence over the governance of the network.

1. **Practical Byzantine Fault Tolerance (PBFT)**:

- **How PBFT Works**: PBFT is a consensus mechanism designed to improve **fault tolerance** and **scalability**. It works by using a smaller, trusted group of nodes that communicate with each other to agree on the validity of transactions. The system can tolerate up to one-third of the nodes being faulty or malicious without compromising the integrity of the network.
- **Efficiency and Security**: PBFT is often used in **permissioned blockchains**, where the participants are known and trusted. It offers a high level of security and can achieve consensus quickly, but it requires a high level of communication between nodes, which can reduce scalability in large networks.

Summary

Each consensus mechanism comes with its own set of strengths and trade-offs:

- **PoW** is secure but environmentally costly.
- **PoS** is energy-efficient and secure, making it a popular choice for newer blockchains.

- **DPoS** is scalable and democratic but relies on a smaller group of validators.
- **PBFT** is fast and fault-tolerant but works best in permissioned environments.

The choice of consensus mechanism depends on the specific needs of the blockchain, such as **security**, **scalability**, **energy efficiency**, and **decentralization**.

Security in Blockchain

One of the most compelling features of blockchain technology is its **security**. Blockchain uses a combination of **cryptographic hashing**, **digital signatures**, and decentralized protocols to protect data and ensure the integrity of transactions. This makes it a **trustless** system, where users don't need to rely on a central authority for validation or verification. In this section, we'll explore how **cryptographic hashing** ensures the integrity of data, the role of **digital signatures** in securing transactions, and how blockchain prevents **double-spending** and **fraud**.

Cryptographic Hashing and How It Ensures Data Integrity

Cryptographic hashing is the process of transforming data into a fixed-length string of characters, typically a series of numbers and letters, through a mathematical algorithm. In blockchain, each block contains a **hash** of the previous block, creating a **chain** of blocks, which is why the technology is called "blockchain."

1. **How Hashing Works**:

- When a block is created, its data (including transaction details and previous block's hash) is passed through a **hashing algorithm** (such as SHA-256).
- The algorithm produces a **unique output**—a fixed-length string of characters called a **hash**. Even the slightest change in the input data will result in a completely different hash, ensuring that data cannot be tampered with.
- Each new block contains the hash of the previous block, creating a **chain of blocks**. This means that if someone tries to alter any block's data (for example, by changing a transaction), the hash will change, and the tampering will be immediately detectable.

1. **Ensuring Data Integrity**:

- Because each block is linked to the previous one through its hash, altering data in a block would change the hash, breaking the chain. This makes blockchain **immutable**—once data is recorded, it cannot be changed or deleted without invalidating the entire chain.
- This **cryptographic security** prevents unauthorized changes to the blockchain, ensuring that the data remains **tamper-proof** and **trustworthy**.

Digital Signatures and Their Role in Security

Digital signatures are another essential component of blockchain security. They use **asymmetric cryptography** to verify the authenticity of transactions and ensure that only the rightful owner can sign and authorize a transaction.

1. **How Digital Signatures Work**:

- When a user wants to send cryptocurrency, they sign the transaction with their **private key**, creating a digital signature. This signature proves that the transaction was initiated by the owner of the corresponding **public key** (i.e., the wallet address).
- The **public key** is made available to the network, while the **private key** is kept secret. Anyone with the public key can verify the authenticity of the digital signature, but only the holder of the private key can create a valid signature.

1. **Ensuring Security**:

- Digital signatures ensure that the **integrity** and **authenticity** of transactions are preserved. If someone tries to alter a transaction after it has been signed, the signature will no longer be valid.
- This prevents **fraudulent transactions** and guarantees that only the legitimate owner of the assets can authorize a transfer.

How Blockchain Prevents Double-Spending and Fraud

One of the most significant challenges in digital currency is preventing **double-spending**—the act of spending the same digital asset more than once. Blockchain solves this problem using its decentralized nature and the mechanisms of consensus and validation.

1. **Preventing Double-Spending**:

- In traditional digital payments, a central authority (like a bank or payment processor) keeps track of the balance in an account and ensures that funds are only spent once. In a decentralized system like blockchain, there is no central authority.
- Instead, the network of nodes **consensus mechanisms** (like **Proof of Work** or **Proof of Stake**) work to ensure that only one valid transaction is recorded on the blockchain. When a user tries to spend the same cryptocurrency twice, the network will reject the second transaction because the asset has already been spent and recorded in the blockchain.

1. **How Blockchain Prevents Fraud**:

- Blockchain's **immutability** and **transparency** ensure that once a transaction is recorded, it cannot be altered or deleted. This prevents fraud, as malicious actors cannot simply erase or modify transaction histories.
- Additionally, the **public ledger** allows anyone to verify the validity of transactions, making it difficult for fraudulent activity to go unnoticed.
- With **digital signatures**, only the owner of the cryptocurrency can initiate a transaction, further reducing the likelihood of fraud.

Summary

Blockchain technology leverages cryptographic principles like **hashing** and **digital signatures** to ensure the security of transactions and prevent fraud. The use of **consensus mechanisms** ensures that only valid transactions are recorded, preventing double-spending and making it impossible for malicious actors to manipulate the blockchain. This combination of features makes blockchain a **trustless**, **secure**, and **immutable** platform for exchanging value and data.

2.2 Cryptocurrency Transactions and Wallets

How Cryptocurrency Transactions Work

Cryptocurrency transactions are a dynamic process that ensures the secure and transparent transfer of digital assets between users. From initiating a transaction to its confirmation on the blockchain, every step involves various key elements working together, including **wallets**, **addresses**, **miners**, **validators**, and **transaction fees**. This section will break down the core steps involved in sending and receiving cryptocurrency, the role of miners and validators in confirming transactions, and the importance of transaction fees.

Steps Involved in Sending and Receiving Crypto

1. **Setting Up a Wallet**:

- A cryptocurrency wallet is essential for holding and managing digital assets. It consists of a **public key** (your wallet address) and a **private key** (used to sign transactions).

- **Public key**: This serves as the **address** where you receive cryptocurrency.
- **Private key**: This is a secret key that you use to **authorize** transactions and prove ownership of your digital assets.

1. **Initiating a Transaction**:

- To send cryptocurrency, the sender must:
- Open their wallet and select the **recipient's public address**.
- Enter the **amount** they want to send.
- **Sign the transaction** with their private key to prove they own the funds and authorize the transfer.

1. **Broadcasting the Transaction**:

- Once signed, the transaction is broadcast to the network, where it is sent to the **nodes** (computers running the blockchain software) for validation.
- The transaction is temporarily in a **pool** of unconfirmed transactions (called the **mempool** in some blockchains), waiting to be added to a block.

1. **Transaction Confirmation**:

- **Miners** (in Proof of Work systems) or **validators** (in Proof of Stake systems) validate the transaction to ensure its legitimacy.
- They check if the sender has sufficient funds, if the transaction is properly signed, and if it complies with

network rules.

- Once the transaction is validated, it is grouped with others into a **block**, which is then added to the blockchain.
- This process is a key feature of the blockchain's **decentralized** nature.

1. **Receiving the Transaction**:

- After the transaction is confirmed and added to the blockchain, the recipient's wallet reflects the updated balance.
- The recipient can view their **transaction history**, which shows all previous transactions (both incoming and outgoing).

The Role of Miners and Validators in Confirming Transactions

Miners and **validators** are the backbone of the blockchain's consensus mechanism, ensuring that only legitimate transactions are recorded.

1. **Miners** (Proof of Work):

- In **Proof of Work (PoW)** blockchains (like Bitcoin), miners compete to solve complex cryptographic puzzles. The first miner to solve the puzzle adds the block of validated transactions to the blockchain.
- Miners must validate each transaction to ensure that the sender has sufficient funds and that there is no fraud (e.g., double-spending).

- Miners are rewarded with newly minted cryptocurrency (such as Bitcoin) and **transaction fees** for their work in confirming and securing the network.

1. **Validators** (Proof of Stake):

- In **Proof of Stake (PoS)** blockchains (like Ethereum 2.0), **validators** are chosen based on the amount of cryptocurrency they have "staked" as collateral.
- Validators validate and propose blocks based on their stake and the protocol rules, confirming the legitimacy of the transactions within the block.
- In PoS systems, validators are incentivized by **block rewards** and **transaction fees**, and are penalized for acting maliciously (e.g., by validating fraudulent transactions).

Transaction Fees and Their Importance

Transaction fees are a key part of the cryptocurrency ecosystem, playing several important roles in maintaining a secure and functional network.

1. **Incentivizing Miners/Validators**:

- Transaction fees act as **incentives** for miners and validators to confirm and add transactions to the blockchain.
- Miners in PoW systems and validators in PoS systems are rewarded with fees in addition to block rewards for confirming transactions.
- Higher transaction fees can prioritize transactions in a congested network. For instance, users willing to pay

higher fees may see their transactions confirmed faster during periods of high demand.

1. **Network Efficiency**:

- Transaction fees help manage **network congestion**. In times of high transaction volumes, users can pay higher fees to ensure their transaction is included in the next block.
- The inclusion of fees also helps **limit spam transactions** on the network, ensuring that only legitimate transactions are processed.

1. **Security**:

- Fees contribute to the **security** of the network by rewarding miners and validators for maintaining the blockchain. This incentivizes them to secure the network and act in the best interests of the system.
- In PoW systems, miners use computational resources to validate and confirm transactions, and transaction fees help compensate for the high energy costs involved. In PoS, validators are rewarded for honest validation of transactions.

1. **Fee Structure**:

- Transaction fees can vary depending on the blockchain's demand, the size of the transaction, and network conditions.
- **Base fees** are typically set by the network, and users can

choose to add an **additional tip** to ensure faster processing of their transaction.

Summary

In summary, cryptocurrency transactions involve several key steps: initiating the transaction from a wallet, broadcasting it to the network, validating it through mining or staking, and confirming the transaction on the blockchain. **Miners** and **validators** play essential roles in confirming transactions and maintaining the network's integrity. **Transaction fees** incentivize these actors to prioritize and confirm transactions, ensuring the network's security and efficiency.

Types of Wallets

When dealing with cryptocurrencies, a **wallet** is essential for storing, sending, and receiving digital assets. However, not all wallets are the same. They can be categorized into two broad types: **hot wallets** and **cold wallets**. Each has its own set of advantages and security considerations. In this section, we'll explore the differences between these wallet types, the importance of **private keys**, and how to securely **back up** and **recover** your wallet.

Hot Wallets vs. Cold Wallets

1. **Hot Wallets**:

- **Hot wallets** are software-based wallets that are connected to the internet. These wallets are more convenient for users who need quick access to their funds for frequent transactions.
- **Examples**:
- **Software wallets** installed on a computer (e.g., Exodus, Electrum).
- **Mobile apps** that allow you to store and manage your cryptocurrency on smartphones (e.g., Trust Wallet, Meta-Mask).
- **Advantages**:
- Fast and easy access to your cryptocurrency for everyday use.
- Ideal for users who need to make frequent transactions or participate in decentralized finance (DeFi) applications.
- **Disadvantages**:
- More vulnerable to **hacking** and malware because they are connected to the internet.
- Private keys are stored digitally and can be compromised if the device is infected or if the wallet provider is hacked.

1. **Cold Wallets**:

- **Cold wallets** are offline storage solutions, making them far more secure than hot wallets. These wallets store private keys offline, protecting them from online threats.

- **Examples**:
- **Hardware wallets** (e.g., Ledger Nano S, Trezor) are physical devices used to store private keys securely offline.
- **Advantages**:
- Highly secure, as they are **not connected to the internet**, making them resistant to hacking attempts and online threats.
- Suitable for long-term storage of cryptocurrency (also known as "cold storage").
- **Disadvantages**:
- Less convenient for frequent transactions, as you need to physically connect the device to a computer or mobile phone to access your funds.
- Requires more effort to set up and manage.

The Importance of Securing Your Wallet and Private Keys

Regardless of whether you use a hot or cold wallet, the security of your wallet hinges on **securing your private keys**. The **private key** is the cryptographic key that gives you control over your cryptocurrency and allows you to sign transactions.

- **Private Key**:
- The private key is the most critical piece of information in your wallet. If someone gains access to your private key, they can spend your cryptocurrency and transfer it to their own wallet.
- **Never share your private key**. Anyone who has access to it can take control of your funds.

- **Public Key**:
- The public key (or address) is like your bank account number. It is meant to be shared, as it is used to receive funds.
- **Important Note**: While the public key can be freely shared, the private key must always remain private and secure.

Wallet Recovery and Backup Methods

Losing access to your wallet or private keys can result in the permanent loss of your cryptocurrency. Therefore, it's critical to have proper **backup** and **recovery** methods in place. Most wallets, whether hot or cold, provide methods to back up and restore your wallet if necessary.

1. **Backup**:

- **Seed Phrase** (Recovery Phrase):
- Most wallets generate a **12-24 word seed phrase** during setup. This is the master key to your wallet and can be used to recover access to your cryptocurrency if your wallet is lost or the device is damaged.
- **Store the seed phrase** in a safe, offline location (e.g., a physical piece of paper, a metal backup, or an encrypted offline device).
- **Important**: Never store your seed phrase digitally (e.g., in an email or on a cloud storage service) as it can be hacked or compromised.

1. **Recovery**:

71

- In the event you lose access to your wallet or private keys, you can restore access by entering the seed phrase into the wallet's recovery system.
- **Cold Wallet Recovery**: If using a hardware wallet, you can recover your wallet on a new device by entering your seed phrase.
- **Hot Wallet Recovery**: Most mobile apps and software wallets allow you to recover your wallet using the seed phrase if you lose access to the app or your device.

Summary

In summary, **hot wallets** and **cold wallets** serve different purposes in the world of cryptocurrency. Hot wallets provide easy, fast access to funds for frequent use, while cold wallets offer a higher level of security for long-term storage. **Private keys** must be securely stored and protected, and having a reliable **backup** method, such as a **seed phrase**, is essential to ensure you can always recover access to your funds.

Exchanges and Trading

Cryptocurrency exchanges are essential platforms that enable users to **buy**, **sell**, and **trade** digital assets. Whether you are a beginner or an experienced trader, understanding how these exchanges work, the difference between **centralized** and **decentralized exchanges**, and how to set up an account on major exchanges (e.g., **Coinbase**, **Binance**) is crucial. This section will explain how exchanges facilitate crypto transactions, the distinction between the two types of exchanges, and how to get started with setting up an account.

How Cryptocurrency Exchanges Work

Cryptocurrency exchanges are online platforms that facilitate the exchange of digital assets between buyers and sellers. Here's how they generally work:

1. **Buying and Selling**:

- Users can purchase cryptocurrencies using traditional **fiat currencies** (e.g., USD, EUR) or other **cryptocurrencies** (e.g., Bitcoin, Ethereum).
- To buy or sell, you create an order on the exchange. You can either place a **market order** (buy/sell immediately at the current market price) or a **limit order** (buy/sell at a specified price).
- Once the order is matched with a seller or buyer, the transaction is completed, and the cryptocurrency is transferred to the buyer's wallet (or exchange wallet if the buyer does not withdraw the funds).

1. **Trading**:

- Exchanges also offer a **trading platform** where users can speculate on the price movements of various cryptocurrencies. This includes spot trading, margin trading, and derivatives trading.
- **Spot trading** refers to the buying and selling of actual cryptocurrencies, while **margin trading** allows users to borrow funds to trade larger positions. **Derivatives**

trading allows traders to buy and sell contracts based on the price of cryptocurrencies without owning the underlying asset.

1. **Fees**:

- Exchanges charge fees for transactions, which can vary depending on the platform and the type of transaction. **Trading fees** typically range from 0.1% to 1% per trade. Some exchanges also charge **deposit/withdrawal fees** for transferring funds in and out of the platform.

Centralized vs. Decentralized Exchanges

1. **Centralized Exchanges (CEX)**:

- **Centralized exchanges** (e.g., **Coinbase**, **Binance**, **Kraken**) are third-party platforms that act as intermediaries between buyers and sellers. These platforms store user funds in **custodial wallets** and manage the order books.
- **Advantages**:
- **User-friendly** with easy-to-use interfaces.
- Provide a variety of trading pairs and high liquidity.
- Faster transactions and support for fiat currency deposits and withdrawals.
- **Disadvantages**:
- Users must trust the exchange with their funds, exposing them to risks of **hacking**, **fraud**, or exchange failure.
- Exchange fees can be higher than decentralized platforms.

1. **Decentralized Exchanges (DEX)**:

- **Decentralized exchanges** (e.g., **Uniswap**, **SushiSwap**, **PancakeSwap**) operate without a central authority. Instead of a third-party intermediary, trades occur directly between users (peer-to-peer) through **smart contracts**.
- **Advantages**:
- **Enhanced privacy** since users control their private keys and funds.
- Lower fees, as there are no intermediaries.
- Less risk of exchange failure or hacking since there is no central entity controlling the funds.
- **Disadvantages**:
- **Lower liquidity** compared to centralized exchanges.
- Can be more complex to use, especially for beginners.
- Limited options for fiat-to-crypto trading, as DEXs usually support only **crypto-to-crypto** trades.

How to Set Up Accounts on Major Exchanges

Setting up an account on a major exchange like **Coinbase** or **Binance** is a straightforward process. Here's an overview:

1. **Coinbase**:

- **Sign Up**: Visit the Coinbase website or download the Coinbase app and create a new account using your email address.
- **Verify Identity**: Complete the **KYC (Know Your Customer)** process by submitting a photo ID (passport, driver's license, etc.).

- **Link Payment Method**: Connect a **bank account**, **credit card**, or **debit card** to fund your account. You can also deposit cryptocurrency if you already own some.
- **Buy/Sell Cryptocurrency**: Once your account is set up, you can start buying, selling, or storing cryptocurrency in your **Coinbase wallet**.

1. **Binance**:

- **Sign Up**: Visit Binance's website and register with an email address. You may need to enable **two-factor authentication** for added security.
- **Verify Identity**: Complete the **KYC** process by uploading your ID and verifying your identity.
- **Deposit Funds**: You can deposit cryptocurrency or link a **bank account** or **payment card** to deposit fiat currency.
- **Start Trading**: Once your account is verified and funded, you can start trading on Binance. Choose from a wide range of cryptocurrencies and trading pairs.

Summary

Cryptocurrency exchanges facilitate the buying, selling, and trading of digital currencies. **Centralized exchanges (CEX)** offer user-friendly platforms with high liquidity and fiat options, but require trust in a third party to manage funds. **Decentralized exchanges (DEX)** provide greater privacy and lower fees, but can be more complex and have lower liquidity. To get started, you can set up an account on major exchanges like **Coinbase** or **Binance**, providing your ID for verification and linking a payment method for deposits and withdrawals.

2.3 Understanding Smart Contracts

What are Smart Contracts?

A **smart contract** is a self-executing agreement where the terms of the contract are written directly into **code** on the blockchain. These digital contracts automatically execute, control, and document the performance of an agreement without requiring intermediaries like lawyers or notaries. This section will break down what smart contracts are, how they eliminate intermediaries, and explore some of their most exciting **use cases** across various industries.

Self-Executing Contracts with Terms Written into Code

1. **What is a Smart Contract?**

- A smart contract is a digital contract that **automatically executes** actions when predefined conditions are met. The terms of the contract are written in the form of **computer code** on a blockchain, and these terms are immutable (they cannot be altered once deployed).
- Once a condition is fulfilled, the contract automatically triggers the next step of the process without human intervention.

1. **How Smart Contracts Work**:

- A **trigger** (event or condition) initiates the smart contract.

- The contract's **conditions** are checked and executed by the **blockchain network** (using nodes, miners, or validators).
- Once the conditions are satisfied, the contract's **actions** are performed—such as transferring cryptocurrency, updating a ledger, or executing another contract—without the need for third-party approval.
- For example, a smart contract for buying a house might automatically transfer ownership of the property once the buyer's payment is confirmed.

1. **Code-Based Logic**:

- Smart contracts are written using programming languages like **Solidity** (the most common language for Ethereum smart contracts).
- The contract code contains **if/then** logic, where certain actions occur only when specific conditions are met.

How Smart Contracts Eliminate Intermediaries

1. **Traditional Contracts vs. Smart Contracts**:

- In traditional contracts, third-party intermediaries—such as lawyers, notaries, or brokers—are typically involved to ensure that both parties meet the terms of the agreement.
- Smart contracts, by contrast, **remove the need for intermediaries** because they are automatically enforced by code and the blockchain network itself.

1. **Advantages of Eliminating Intermediaries**:

- **Faster Transactions**: With smart contracts, execution happens immediately once conditions are met, without waiting for human intervention or business hours.
- **Lower Costs**: Eliminating intermediaries means fewer fees associated with transaction verification, paperwork, and administrative tasks.
- **Increased Security**: The blockchain provides a secure and transparent environment where actions cannot be tampered with or altered once they're executed.
- **Improved Trust**: Since the contract code is visible and executed by the network, all parties can trust the terms of the contract without relying on a third party.

Use Cases of Smart Contracts

Smart contracts have a wide array of use cases across industries, offering transformative potential for sectors like **real estate**, **insurance**, and **finance**, among others.

1. **Real Estate**:

- Smart contracts in real estate can automate property sales and leases.
- For example, when a buyer makes a payment, a smart contract could automatically transfer the property title to the buyer and update the records on the blockchain.
- **Benefits**: This eliminates the need for lawyers and no-taries, speeds up the process, and reduces costs associated with paperwork and delays.

1. **Insurance**:

- In the insurance industry, smart contracts can automate claims processing.
- For example, in **flight delay insurance**, a smart contract could automatically trigger compensation payouts to policyholders if a flight is delayed by more than a certain time, without requiring an agent to process the claim.
- **Benefits**: Faster payouts, fewer fraud cases, and reduced administrative costs.

1. **Supply Chain Management**:

- Smart contracts can help automate the verification of goods in transit.
- For instance, a smart contract could automatically release payment for goods once they've been delivered and verified to meet specific quality standards, which is tracked on the blockchain.
- **Benefits**: Transparency, security, and automation of multi-step processes.

1. **Finance and Banking**:

- In the finance industry, smart contracts are used for things like **automated loan agreements**, **decentralized finance (DeFi)** protocols, and **cross-border payments**.
- Smart contracts can automatically execute financial agreements like loan disbursements or margin calls without the need for banks or brokers to intervene.
- **Benefits**: Reduced reliance on traditional financial institutions, lower fees, and faster transaction execution.

1. **Voting Systems**:

- In government or corporate voting systems, smart contracts can ensure that votes are recorded securely and transparently, and that election results are immediately verified once the voting period ends.
- **Benefits**: Secure, tamper-proof records, and faster counting.

Summary

Smart contracts represent a significant innovation by automating agreements and transactions in a secure, transparent, and tamper-proof environment. By eliminating the need for intermediaries and automating processes, smart contracts reduce costs, speed up transactions, and increase trust. They are already being applied in industries like **real estate**, **insurance**, **supply chain management**, and **finance**, with the potential to revolutionize countless other sectors in the coming years.

How Smart Contracts Work

Smart contracts are self-executing agreements with the terms of the contract directly written into code. The contract automatically enforces and executes the terms when certain predefined conditions are met. The power of smart contracts lies in their ability to operate without intermediaries, which streamlines processes, reduces costs, and ensures trust between parties. However, as powerful as they are, smart contracts come with certain risks and security concerns that must be addressed carefully.

81

In this section, we'll explore how smart contracts are triggered, the role of **Ethereum** in the smart contract ecosystem, and common **security pitfalls** that developers must guard against.

Trigger-Based Execution and Conditional Agreements

1. **Trigger-Based Execution**:

- Smart contracts are **triggered** by specific conditions or events. These conditions are written into the contract's code using **if/then logic**. For example, a smart contract could be set up to transfer funds once a buyer sends a payment.
- **Trigger types**:
- **External triggers**: These can be external events or data feeds, such as receiving payment on the blockchain, or a temperature sensor indicating a certain threshold.
- **Internal triggers**: These refer to events within the blockchain network itself, such as the successful mining of a block or the completion of another smart contract.
- Once the trigger condition is met, the contract executes the next step without requiring human intervention. This can involve transferring funds, updating records, or even executing additional smart contracts.

1. **Conditional Agreements**:

- Smart contracts use **conditional statements** to define the terms of the agreement. For instance, the contract could state: "If the buyer deposits 5 ETH into the contract, then the seller will transfer ownership of the property."

- These conditions are based on real-world actions or data, and they must be fulfilled for the contract to execute the next step. The contract itself cannot execute actions that go beyond the coded conditions.
- **Example**: A smart contract could be used in a **flight delay insurance** policy, where the contract only pays out when the flight is delayed by a certain amount, and the trigger for that could be an official flight database.

Ethereum's Role in the Smart Contract Ecosystem

1. **Ethereum and Smart Contracts**:

- **Ethereum** is the most widely used blockchain for deploying smart contracts. It was the first platform to introduce **programmable blockchain** capabilities, allowing developers to write decentralized applications (dApps) using **smart contracts**.
- Ethereum uses a **Turing-complete language** called **Solidity** to write smart contracts, enabling the execution of complex logic on the blockchain.
- **Ethereum Virtual Machine (EVM)** is the decentralized computing environment that executes the code of smart contracts. It allows any node in the network to run the same code and ensure consistency across the system.

1. **Key Features of Ethereum's Smart Contracts**:

- **Decentralization**: Ethereum smart contracts are hosted on the Ethereum blockchain, which is decentralized and operates without a central authority.

- **Immutability**: Once a smart contract is deployed, it cannot be changed, ensuring trust and transparency. If the contract is written correctly, it will execute as intended.
- **Security**: Ethereum's network security protects the integrity of smart contracts by using **cryptographic hashing** and the consensus mechanism of **Proof of Work** (PoW) or **Proof of Stake** (PoS), which ensures that contract execution is tamper-proof.

1. **Ethereum's Ecosystem**:

- Ethereum is more than just a blockchain; it has a thriving **ecosystem** of decentralized finance (DeFi) applications, NFT marketplaces, and other dApps that rely heavily on smart contracts. Major platforms like **Uniswap**, **MakerDAO**, and **Aave** use Ethereum's smart contracts to facilitate decentralized financial services.

Security Concerns and Common Pitfalls

While smart contracts offer a range of benefits, they also come with their share of **security concerns** and potential pitfalls, especially given that they are immutable once deployed and often involve significant amounts of money. Some common issues include:

1. **Coding Errors**:

- Since smart contracts are written in code, errors in the code can lead to unintended behavior. A poorly written contract can result in **loss of funds** or **contract exploits**.

- Example: **The DAO hack** in 2016, where a vulnerability in a smart contract led to the theft of over $50 million in Ethereum. A flaw in the code allowed attackers to repeatedly withdraw funds before they were locked in the contract.

1. **Reentrancy Attacks**:

- This type of attack occurs when a contract calls another contract, and the second contract calls back to the first before the first contract finishes its execution. This can result in unintended behavior, such as the unauthorized transfer of funds.
- Example: The **The DAO hack** also involved a reentrancy attack, where attackers exploited the contract's inability to handle multiple calls properly.

1. **Gas Limit Issues**:

- Every operation on Ethereum requires **gas** (computational resources). A smart contract that is too complex or inefficient may run out of gas, causing the contract to fail or become stuck.
- Developers need to carefully manage **gas usage** to ensure that their contract can execute without running out of funds for gas.

1. **Immutability and Bugs**:

- Once deployed, smart contracts cannot be altered. If there is a bug in the contract after it's been deployed, there is no easy way to fix it.

- Some platforms, like **Upgradable Smart Contracts** on Ethereum, allow developers to deploy new versions of smart contracts, but this comes with added complexity and risks.

1. **Lack of External Validation**:

- Many smart contracts rely on **oracles**—external services that provide real-world data (like the current price of an asset or the outcome of an event). If the oracle is compromised, the contract may execute based on false data.

Summary

Smart contracts are self-executing agreements that automatically carry out the terms of a contract based on predefined conditions. Ethereum is the leading blockchain for smart contract development, providing a decentralized platform that allows complex applications to run securely. However, the technology is not without risks—coding errors, security vulnerabilities like **reentrancy attacks**, and issues with **gas limits** and **external oracles** can cause problems if not properly managed. Developers must be diligent in testing and auditing smart contracts to avoid costly mistakes.

Popular Platforms for Smart Contracts

As blockchain technology continues to evolve, a variety of platforms have emerged to support the development and execution of **smart contracts**. These platforms provide the infrastructure that allows developers to build decentralized applications (dApps) and decentralized finance (DeFi) solutions that operate securely, efficiently, and without intermediaries. In this section, we'll explore some of the **most popular smart contract platforms**, how they support **DeFi** and **dApps**, and what makes them unique.

Ethereum: The Pioneer of Smart Contracts

1. **Ethereum Overview**:

- **Ethereum** is the first and most well-known platform for smart contracts. It introduced the concept of a **programmable blockchain**, allowing developers to write and deploy decentralized applications (dApps) using **smart contracts**.
- Ethereum uses the **Solidity** programming language, which enables developers to create complex contract logic and execute it on the Ethereum **Virtual Machine (EVM)**.
- The Ethereum ecosystem has grown to become home to a vast array of **DeFi applications**, such as **Uniswap**, **Aave**, and **Compound**, and other dApps like **NFT marketplaces** and **Decentralized Autonomous Organizations (DAOs)**.

1. **Ethereum's Unique Features**:

- **Decentralization**: Ethereum operates on a decentralized blockchain, where the consensus mechanism (formerly **Proof of Work**, now transitioning to **Proof of Stake**) ensures that no single entity controls the network.
- **Security**: The network is highly secure, with the Ethereum Foundation constantly working to improve scalability, security, and energy efficiency.

Binance Smart Chain (BSC): Fast and Low-Cost

1. **Binance Smart Chain Overview**:

- **Binance Smart Chain (BSC)** is a blockchain network developed by **Binance**, one of the world's largest cryptocurrency exchanges. BSC aims to provide a high-performance blockchain that is **compatible with Ethereum** but is designed to offer **faster transactions** and **lower fees**.
- BSC uses **Proof of Staked Authority (PoSA)** as its consensus mechanism, enabling it to process transactions quickly with low costs.

1. **BSC's Role in DeFi**:

- BSC has become a popular platform for **DeFi applications** due to its low transaction fees and fast confirmation times. Major projects like **PancakeSwap**, **Venus**, and **BakerySwap** have been built on BSC.
- BSC's compatibility with Ethereum's ecosystem means that developers can easily port their **Ethereum dApps** to BSC to take advantage of its lower fees and faster transaction times.

Solana: Speed and Scalability

1. **Solana Overview**:

- **Solana** is a high-performance blockchain known for its **extremely fast transaction speeds** and **low fees**. Solana uses a unique consensus mechanism called **Proof of History (PoH)**, combined with **Proof of Stake (PoS)**, to achieve rapid transaction processing without sacrificing decentralization.
- Solana's **scalability** makes it an attractive option for DeFi applications and large-scale dApps.

1. **Solana's DeFi Ecosystem**:

- Solana has attracted a number of innovative DeFi projects like **Raydium**, **Serum**, and **Saber** due to its scalability and low transaction costs.
- Solana's ability to handle thousands of transactions per second (TPS) makes it an ideal platform for high-volume DeFi protocols, as well as **NFT marketplaces** and **gaming dApps**.

Other Notable Platforms for Smart Contracts

1. **Cardano**:

- **Cardano** is another blockchain platform that aims to offer a more sustainable and scalable alternative to Ethereum.

Cardano uses a **Proof of Stake (PoS)** consensus mechanism and features a highly secure and energy-efficient design.

- Cardano's **Alonzo upgrade** introduced **smart contract functionality**, enabling developers to build decentralized applications on the Cardano blockchain.

1. **Polkadot**:

- **Polkadot** enables the interoperability of multiple blockchains by allowing them to communicate and share data with one another. This is achieved through its **Relay Chain** and **Parachains**.
- Polkadot's unique approach to scalability and cross-chain compatibility has made it a rising star for DeFi and smart contract-based applications.

1. **Tezos**:

- **Tezos** is a smart contract platform that focuses on self-amending blockchain technology. Tezos uses **Liquid Proof of Stake (LPoS)** and allows the blockchain to evolve and update without hard forks.
- Tezos supports DeFi applications and is known for its emphasis on **on-chain governance**, allowing the community to vote on changes to the protocol.

1. **Avalanche**:

- **Avalanche** is another high-performance blockchain platform that is designed to be scalable, fast, and secure. It uses a **consensus protocol** called **Avalanche consensus** to achieve high throughput.
- Avalanche has attracted a growing ecosystem of DeFi applications due to its low-cost transactions and quick finality.

Decentralized Finance (DeFi) Applications

1. **What is DeFi?**

- **DeFi** refers to a set of financial services—such as lending, borrowing, trading, and yield farming—that are built on blockchain platforms using smart contracts. These services operate without intermediaries like banks or financial institutions.
- DeFi applications are typically built on top of **Ethereum**, **Binance Smart Chain**, **Solana**, and other smart contract platforms.

1. **Examples of DeFi Applications**:

- **Decentralized Exchanges (DEXs)**: Platforms like **Uniswap** (Ethereum), **PancakeSwap** (BSC), and **Raydium** (Solana) allow users to trade cryptocurrencies directly from their wallets without relying on centralized exchanges.
- **Lending and Borrowing**: Platforms like **Compound** (Ethereum) and **Aave** (Ethereum) enable users to lend their assets in exchange for interest, or borrow assets with

collateral, all governed by smart contracts.

- **Stablecoins**: DeFi platforms also facilitate the creation and use of **stablecoins**, such as **DAI** and **USDC**, which are pegged to the value of traditional currencies like the U.S. dollar, allowing for more stable transactions.

Decentralized Applications (dApps)

1. **What Are dApps?**

- **dApps** are applications that run on decentralized networks, usually with no central point of control. They utilize **smart contracts** to execute their operations and are typically open-source, meaning that their code is available to the public for verification.
- dApps can serve a wide variety of use cases, from **finance** (DeFi apps) to **gaming** (NFT platforms, blockchain-based games) and **social networking** (decentralized social media).

1. **Examples of Popular dApps**:

- **Uniswap** (Ethereum): A decentralized exchange that allows users to swap Ethereum-based tokens directly from their wallets.
- **Opensea** (Ethereum): A decentralized marketplace for trading **NFTs** (Non-Fungible Tokens).
- **Axie Infinity** (Ethereum and Ronin): A blockchain-based game that allows users to earn through in-game assets and tokens.

Summary

The world of smart contracts is rapidly evolving, and numerous blockchain platforms are leading the charge in enabling decentralized applications and financial services. **Ethereum** remains the pioneer of smart contract platforms, but other platforms like **Binance Smart Chain**, **Solana**, **Cardano**, and **Polkadot** are offering unique advantages such as faster transactions, lower fees, and increased scalability. The emergence of **DeFi** and **dApps** is reshaping industries like finance, gaming, and digital art, and these platforms are at the heart of this transformation.

Chapter 3: Real-World Applications of Blockchain and Cryptocurrencies

3.1 Blockchain in Finance: The Rise of DeFi

What is Decentralized Finance (DeFi)?

Decentralized Finance (DeFi) represents a new way of delivering financial services that eliminates the need for intermediaries like banks, brokers, and traditional financial institutions. By leveraging blockchain technology and smart contracts, DeFi platforms allow users to access a broad range of financial services in a peer-to-peer (P2P) environment. This model offers enhanced transparency, security, and accessibility while reducing costs and increasing control for users.

In this section, we will break down the key elements of **DeFi**, including **lending**, **borrowing**, **yield farming**, **staking**, and explore some of the most popular DeFi platforms like **Uniswap**, **Aave**, and **Compound**.

Peer-to-Peer Financial Services Without Intermediaries

1. Peer-to-Peer (P2P) Finance:

- Traditional financial systems rely on centralized inter-mediaries banks, brokers, and exchanges—to facilitate transactions and services like lending, borrowing, and trading. In contrast, **Defi** platforms eliminate these intermediaries by using **smart contracts** to facilitate transactions directly between users.
- **Smart contracts** automatically enforce the terms of agreements between parties, reducing the need for trust in intermediaries and ensuring that financial services are transparent and secure.
- In **Defi**, users maintain control over their funds, with transactions occurring on decentralized platforms like **Ethereum, Binance Smart Chain**, and **Solana**.

1. Key Features of Defi:

- **Open and Permissionless**: Defi platforms are open to anyone with an internet connection, without the need for intermediaries, credit checks, or approvals.
- **Transparency and Security**: All transactions and smart contract code are publicly accessible on the blockchain, offering full transparency and reducing the risk of fraud and manipulation.
- **Decentralization**: Defi platforms do not rely on centralized entities, meaning they are less vulnerable to censorship, government intervention, or control by financial institutions.

Lending, Borrowing, Yield Farming, and Staking

1. **Lending and Borrowing**:

- **Lending**: DeFi platforms allow users to lend their cryptocurrency to others in exchange for interest. Unlike traditional loans, these loans are collateralized by cryptocurrency assets and facilitated by smart contracts.
- **Borrowing**: Users can also borrow funds against their crypto holdings, using collateral to secure the loan. If the borrower fails to repay, the collateral is liquidated, ensuring the lender is protected.
- Examples of DeFi lending platforms: **Aave, Compound, MakerDAO**.

1. **Yield Farming**:

- **Yield farming** refers to the process of using cryptocurrency holdings to earn additional tokens or rewards. Users can participate by providing liquidity to DeFi platforms, which in turn use their funds for lending or other financial services.
- In exchange for providing liquidity, users earn **yield**—usually in the form of governance tokens or interest.
- Yield farming can be highly profitable but comes with risks, including **impermanent loss** (the risk that the value of the deposited assets may change in an unfavorable direction).

1. **Staking**:

- **Staking** involves locking up cryptocurrency in a

blockchain network to help secure the network and participate in its consensus mechanism. In return for staking their assets, users receive rewards, often in the form of additional tokens.

- **Proof of Stake (PoS)** blockchains like **Ethereum 2.0** and **Polkadot** offer staking as a way for users to earn passive income while contributing to the security and decentralization of the network.

DeFi Platforms and Protocols

1. **Uniswap**:

- **Uniswap** is a **decentralized exchange (DEX)** that allows users to trade Ethereum-based tokens directly from their wallets without relying on an intermediary. Uniswap uses an **automated market maker (AMM)** model, where users provide liquidity to a pool, and trades occur directly between users and the liquidity pool.
- **Uniswap's token swap** functionality enables users to exchange assets, such as ERC-20 tokens, with minimal fees.

1. **Aave**:

- **Aave** is a **DeFi lending and borrowing platform** that allows users to lend their cryptocurrency and earn interest or borrow funds using crypto as collateral. Aave's platform is built on Ethereum and **Polygon**, and it offers unique features such as **flash loans**—loans that are taken and repaid within a single transaction.

- Aave also allows users to **stake** its native token, **AAVE**, and participate in governance.

1. **Compound**:

- **Compound** is another popular DeFi lending protocol where users can supply and borrow cryptocurrencies. Interest rates on Compound are determined algorithmically, based on supply and demand in the market. Users can earn **COMP tokens** as rewards for providing liquidity.
- Compound has become one of the most well-known DeFi protocols due to its simple user interface and wide range of supported assets.

DeFi Use Cases and Advantages

1. **Financial Inclusion**:

- DeFi is opening up financial services to the **unbanked** and **underbanked** populations around the world. Anyone with an internet connection can access DeFi platforms, regardless of their location, financial history, or access to traditional banking systems.

1. **Lower Fees**:

- By removing intermediaries, DeFi platforms can offer significantly **lower fees** compared to traditional financial systems. Users can access services like lending, borrowing, and trading at a fraction of the cost.

1. **Greater Control**:

- DeFi gives users **full control** over their funds. Unlike traditional banks, which require users to trust third parties with their assets, DeFi allows users to maintain custody of their funds at all times through **smart wallets** and **private keys**.

Summary

Decentralized Finance (DeFi) is revolutionizing the financial industry by enabling a peer-to-peer financial ecosystem without intermediaries. Users can lend, borrow, earn interest through yield farming and staking, and access a wide range of financial services via **DeFi protocols**. Popular platforms like **Uniswap**, **Aave**, and **Compound** are at the forefront of this transformation, providing users with the ability to manage their financial activities directly on the blockchain. With **DeFi**, the financial system becomes more inclusive, transparent, and efficient, offering a promising future for the future of finance.

Advantages of DeFi Over Traditional Finance

Decentralized Finance (DeFi) is rapidly changing the landscape of global finance by offering distinct advantages over traditional financial systems. The core benefits of DeFi lie in its ability to **reduce costs**, **increase access**, and provide

transparency and control to users, all while eliminating the need for intermediaries like banks, brokers, and credit institutions.

In this section, we'll explore the **key advantages** of DeFi over traditional finance, demonstrating how it offers a more efficient, accessible, and user-centric financial ecosystem.

1. Reduced Costs and Faster Transactions

One of the primary benefits of **DeFi** is its ability to **reduce costs** and **speed up transactions** compared to traditional finance.

- **Lower Fees**: Traditional financial systems often involve numerous intermediaries—banks, brokers, payment processors—each of which charges a fee for facilitating services. For example, international money transfers or remittances can take days and incur high fees due to the involvement of banks, currency exchange fees, and processing charges.
- In contrast, **DeFi platforms** reduce these fees significantly by eliminating intermediaries and using blockchain's **smart contracts** to automate transactions directly between users.
- DeFi services like **lending**, **borrowing**, and **trading** come with **lower transaction fees**, making them more cost-effective for users.
- **Faster Transactions**: Traditional financial transactions—especially cross-border payments—can take several business days to clear due to time zone differences, banking hours, and manual processes. In contrast, DeFi platforms

can process transactions **in minutes** or even **seconds**, 24/7, due to their decentralized and automated nature.

- DeFi networks like **Ethereum** and **Binance Smart Chain** allow for **instantaneous transactions** with no need for banks to validate them.

2. Increased Access to Financial Services for the Unbanked

Another significant advantage of **DeFi** over traditional finance is its ability to **increase financial inclusion**.

- **Access for the Unbanked**: An estimated **1.7 billion people** worldwide are **unbanked**, meaning they have no access to traditional banking services such as savings accounts, loans, or credit. Many of these individuals live in remote or underserved regions with limited access to physical banks or financial institutions.
- **DeFi platforms** provide a decentralized, permissionless financial system that allows anyone with an internet connection to access financial services. Users do not need to go through a bank, credit check, or verification process, making **DeFi** highly inclusive.
- With DeFi, anyone with a **smartphone** or **computer** can lend, borrow, trade, or stake assets, without the need for a bank account or approval from a financial institution.
- **Global Accessibility**: DeFi platforms are **borderless**. As long as a person has access to the internet, they can participate in DeFi activities, regardless of their country or region. This is a game-changer for those in developing economies or countries with underdeveloped financial

infrastructures.

3. Transparency and Control for Users

DeFi also offers **greater transparency** and **control** to users compared to traditional finance, empowering individuals in ways that traditional systems cannot.

- **Transparency**: In traditional finance, transactions are typically controlled and recorded by centralized authorities like banks and financial institutions, making it difficult for users to verify or audit the processes. DeFi, on the other hand, is built on **blockchain technology**, which allows **publicly accessible, immutable transaction records**.
- **DeFi platforms** operate in a transparent and open-source manner. Every transaction is recorded on a **public ledger**, meaning anyone can inspect the code or audit the transactions that occur on the network. This ensures **greater accountability** and reduces the risk of fraud or manipulation.
- **Control**: In traditional finance, users have to trust intermediaries (banks, financial institutions, etc.) to manage and control their funds. This creates the potential for fees, delays, or issues with access, especially in times of financial crises or disruptions.
- In the world of **DeFi**, users have **full control** over their assets. They can hold, manage, and transfer their funds without relying on third parties. For example, **DeFi wallets** enable users to store their private keys, ensuring that only they can access their funds, giving them autonomy over their finances.

Summary

In conclusion, DeFi offers **significant advantages** over traditional finance, including:

- **Reduced costs and faster transactions**, thanks to the elimination of intermediaries and the use of blockchain technology for fast and secure transfers.
- **Increased access to financial services** for the **unbanked**, empowering millions of people around the world to participate in global financial systems without the need for banks or credit institutions.
- **Transparency and control** for users, with open and auditable transaction records and the ability to maintain direct control over assets.

These advantages make **DeFi** a powerful tool for financial inclusion, efficiency, and user empowerment, paving the way for a more decentralized and inclusive global financial system.

Challenges and Risks in DeFi

While **DeFi (Decentralized Finance)** offers many revolutionary advantages, it also comes with its own set of **challenges and risks**. As the DeFi ecosystem continues to grow and evolve, these issues need to be addressed to ensure the safety, stability, and sustainability of decentralized financial systems. The primary risks include **smart contract vulnerabilities**, **regulatory uncertainty**, and the inherent **market volatility** that can lead to investor losses.

In this section, we'll explore these challenges in detail and examine the potential risks associated with participating in DeFi platforms.

1. Smart Contract Vulnerabilities and Hacking Risks

- **Smart Contract Bugs and Vulnerabilities**: **Smart contracts** are the backbone of DeFi, enabling decentralized, automated transactions between users. However, smart contracts are only as secure as the code they are written with. **Bugs** or **vulnerabilities** in the code can result in unexpected behaviors, such as the loss of funds or unauthorized access.

- **Coding errors** or poorly written contracts can expose platforms to **exploits**. For example, if a contract contains a bug, it could be exploited by malicious actors to withdraw funds or manipulate outcomes.

- In 2020, the **bZx protocol** was hacked twice due to vulnerabilities in its smart contract code, resulting in significant losses for users.

- **Hacking Attacks**: DeFi platforms are an attractive target for hackers due to their **large amounts of liquidity** and **complex code**. Attackers may exploit weaknesses in smart contracts, blockchain protocols, or even user wallets to gain unauthorized access to funds.

- Examples of major DeFi hacks include the **Yearn Finance hack** in 2020, where an attacker was able to exploit a vulnerability in the platform's smart contract, leading to the theft of over $11 million in cryptocurrency.

2. Regulatory Uncertainty and Compliance Issues

- **Lack of Clear Regulations**: DeFi operates in a **largely unregulated environment**, with little to no oversight from government or financial authorities. This lack of regulation can lead to legal challenges for both users and platforms.
- Many DeFi platforms, especially those involved in lending, borrowing, and token issuance, may fall into **grey areas** of the law, as they often circumvent traditional financial institutions and regulations.
- Regulatory bodies in various countries, such as the **U.S. SEC** or **European financial authorities**, have been slow to establish clear rules for how DeFi should operate. This uncertainty creates **legal risks** for both DeFi platforms and their users.
- **Potential for Future Regulation**: As the DeFi space grows and attracts more attention from both regulators and investors, there is a potential for future **regulation and oversight**. However, this regulatory framework may introduce **compliance costs** for platforms and limit the flexibility that DeFi offers. It could also lead to **increased censorship** or **centralization** if platforms are forced to comply with government rules.

3. Market Volatility and Investor Protection

- **High Market Volatility**: The cryptocurrency markets, and DeFi platforms in particular, are highly **volatile**. Cryptocurrencies are subject to **massive price swings** over short periods, which can lead to substantial financial losses for investors.

- For example, the price of **Bitcoin** or **Ethereum** can fluctuate by 20% or more in a single day, and **DeFi tokens** are often even more volatile. **Flash crashes** or **market manipulation** (e.g., "whale" manipulation) can cause drastic price movements.

- Users participating in DeFi protocols like **yield farming** or **staking** may face significant risks if the value of their collateral drops dramatically, especially in the case of **liquidation events** or **collateral shortfalls**.

- **Investor Protection**: Traditional financial systems have mechanisms in place to protect investors—such as **insurance** on deposits or **consumer protection laws**—which do not yet exist in the DeFi space. DeFi users must assume the risks themselves.

- While some **DeFi platforms** offer **insurance products** or **staking rewards** as incentives, these protections are still in their infancy and often fail to provide full coverage against potential losses due to hacks, market crashes, or platform failures.

Summary

DeFi has the potential to revolutionize global finance, but there are significant **challenges and risks** that need to be addressed:

1. **Smart contract vulnerabilities** pose a significant risk for users, as coding errors or security flaws can lead to large-scale financial losses and hacks.

2. **Regulatory uncertainty** around DeFi raises concerns about the legality and compliance of platforms, with

governments potentially introducing regulations that could limit the decentralized nature of DeFi.

3. **Market volatility** is a key risk for DeFi participants, as cryptocurrency prices are highly unpredictable, which can lead to liquidation events, financial losses, and a lack of investor protection.

While DeFi offers exciting possibilities, users must be aware of these challenges and take precautions, such as conducting thorough research, using **audited platforms**, and employing **secure wallet practices**.

3.2 Blockchain for Supply Chain and Transparency

Supply Chain Tracking and Traceability with Blockchain

One of the most exciting real-world applications of **blockchain technology** is its ability to **transform supply chains**. Traditionally, supply chains have been opaque, prone to errors, and vulnerable to fraud, which can lead to inefficiencies, product recalls, and a lack of trust between buyers and suppliers. **Blockchain** has the potential to address these issues by providing a **transparent**, **immutable**, and **secure** system for tracking goods as they move through every stage of the supply chain—from production and transportation to the point of sale.

In this section, we'll explore **how blockchain enables transparent supply chains**, examine **real-world examples** like **IBM Food Trust** and **VeChain**, and highlight how **blockchain technology** is improving **traceability** to ensure product **authenticity** and **safety**.

1. Blockchain's Role in Creating Transparent Supply Chains

- **Transparency**: Blockchain allows **every transaction** or movement of goods in the supply chain to be recorded on a public, **immutable ledger**. This creates a **transparent record** that can be accessed by all stakeholders in real-time—producers, suppliers, manufacturers, and consumers.
- Each transaction is time-stamped and verified, so no one can alter or tamper with the data. This level of transparency builds **trust** and accountability across the supply chain.
- Blockchain's ability to provide a shared, **immutable ledger** means that all participants can track the **entire history** of a product, from its origin to its final destination.
- **Efficient Tracking**: Blockchain streamlines the **process of tracking goods** by automating the record-keeping through **smart contracts**. This can significantly reduce the time and cost spent on manual tracking systems.
- By using blockchain, **all relevant parties** (from producers to consumers) can track a product's journey across the supply chain, gaining immediate access to real-time updates.

2. Real-World Examples: IBM Food Trust & VeChain

Two prominent examples of **blockchain-based supply chain systems** are **IBM Food Trust** and **VeChain**, both of which have showcased how blockchain can revolutionize the way goods are tracked and verified.

- **IBM Food Trust**: IBM's **Food Trust blockchain** is an example of a **permissioned blockchain** that connects multiple participants across the **food supply chain**—farmers, processors, distributors, retailers, and consumers. Using this system, each player can record key data about the food's journey, such as where it was grown, harvested, and processed, as well as quality checks along the way.

- For example, in the event of a **food recall**, the company can quickly trace the origin of contaminated products, pinpointing the exact source and preventing the spread of harm. This not only enhances **food safety** but also ensures **authenticity** by eliminating counterfeits.

- **Consumers** can scan QR codes on food packaging to see detailed information about the product, including its origin, journey, and quality certifications.

- **VeChain**: VeChain is a **blockchain platform** that focuses on enabling businesses to track products, particularly in sectors like **luxury goods**, **automotive**, and **pharmaceuticals**. VeChain uses **smart chips** and **IoT devices** to record data about products on the blockchain, ensuring that every step of the supply chain is traceable.

- For instance, **luxury goods** like designer handbags can have an embedded **VeChain chip** that allows customers to verify the authenticity of the product by scanning a QR code. This helps combat the problem of **counterfeit goods** and ensures that the product is genuine.

- In the **pharmaceutical industry**, VeChain has been used to ensure that medicines and vaccines maintain the correct storage conditions as they move through the supply chain, thus safeguarding public health and preventing fraud.

3. Tracking Goods from Origin to End-User for Authenticity and Safety

- **Tracking Goods**: Blockchain provides an efficient and reliable way to track goods from **origin to end-user**, ensuring that each stage of the supply chain is recorded, transparent, and verifiable.

- For example, when a consumer buys a product, they can **scan a code** or access the blockchain to verify information about the product's **origin**, **manufacturing**, **shipping**, and **storage conditions**.

- This **end-to-end traceability** is particularly important for **high-value goods** (e.g., luxury items, pharmaceuticals, organic food) where consumers are concerned about authenticity, quality, and safety.

- **Ensuring Safety and Authenticity**: Blockchain can also help in ensuring the **safety** and **authenticity** of goods, particularly in industries where counterfeiting is a concern, such as **pharmaceuticals**, **luxury items**, and **electronics**.

- With blockchain's tamper-proof nature, **counterfeit products** can be easily identified and excluded from the market. Additionally, consumers can be confident that the product they purchase has been stored, transported, and handled according to the required **safety protocols**.

- **Regulatory Compliance**: Blockchain-based traceability also ensures that goods comply with **regulatory standards**. For instance, the **pharmaceutical industry** must adhere to strict regulations on product storage and handling. Blockchain can ensure that these regulations are met, and it provides a **clear audit trail** for regulatory agencies to verify compliance.

Summary

In summary, **blockchain technology** offers a **transparent, secure, and immutable solution** for supply chain tracking and traceability. Key advantages include:

- **Transparency** in every step of the supply chain, from production to end-user, ensuring all parties can verify the authenticity and safety of products.
- **Real-world applications** like **IBM Food Trust** and **VeChain** are already demonstrating the effectiveness of blockchain in improving supply chain management.
- **End-to-end traceability** of goods from origin to the end-user, ensuring **authenticity**, **safety**, and **compliance** with regulatory standards.

Blockchain is paving the way for **smarter**, more **secure**, and **efficient supply chains** that benefit not just businesses but consumers as well, increasing trust in products and reducing fraud.

Blockchain for Provenance and Authentication

One of the most significant benefits of **blockchain technology** is its ability to ensure **provenance** and **authentication** of products. As industries become more globalized, the risks of fraud, counterfeit goods, and lack of transparency have grown. **Blockchain** offers a **secure**, **immutable**, and **transparent** solution to these problems, making it particularly useful for tracking the **authenticity** and **provenance** of high-value items like **luxury goods**, **art**, **diamonds**, and **pharmaceu-**

111

ticals.

This section explores how blockchain technology is being used to prevent fraud, ensure the **quality** of products, and verify the **ownership** and **authenticity** of valuable items. We'll also discuss the role of **Non-Fungible Tokens (NFTs)** in digital and physical goods authentication and provide real-world examples from **luxury goods**, **art**, and **pharmaceuticals**.

1. Ensuring Product Quality and Preventing Fraud in Luxury Goods

- **Counterfeit Luxury Goods**: The market for **luxury goods** such as **designer handbags**, **watches**, and **high-end fashion** is rife with counterfeits. **Blockchain technology** can combat this by providing a **digital certificate of authenticity** for each item, which is recorded on an **immutable ledger**.

- Consumers can use blockchain to verify that the product they're purchasing is genuine. For example, when buying a luxury watch, customers can scan a QR code or enter a unique **ID number** to access its full **provenance history**, showing that it is not a counterfeit.

- Brands like **Louis Vuitton** and **Gucci** are already experimenting with blockchain to provide their customers with a secure way to authenticate their products, reducing the impact of counterfeiting on their businesses.

- **Product Quality Assurance**: Blockchain can also track product quality throughout its lifecycle, ensuring that the goods meet the **standards** set by the manufacturer. For instance, if a luxury handbag is produced with high-quality leather, each step in the process, from the sourcing of the material to the final sale, can be documented and verified via blockchain.

- **Supply chain transparency** provided by blockchain helps verify the integrity and **ethical sourcing** of materials, which is becoming increasingly important to consumers who prioritize sustainability.

2. The Use of NFTs for Verifying Ownership in Art and Collectibles

- **NFTs and Provenance**: **Non-Fungible Tokens (NFTs)**, which represent unique digital assets on the blockchain, are increasingly used to verify **ownership** and **authenticity** in both the digital and physical worlds. NFTs are particularly useful in the context of **art** and **collectibles**, as they provide an immutable record of **provenance** that can be easily tracked and transferred.

- When an artist creates a piece of art, an **NFT** can be minted to represent the original work. The NFT is then linked to the artwork's **blockchain record**, providing a transparent **chain of ownership** and **transaction history**.

- This technology helps address the issue of **art fraud** by verifying the **authenticity** of digital and physical artworks. For example, a **digital painting** could be sold with an accompanying **NFT** that proves its origin, and the buyer would have verifiable proof of ownership, even if the artwork is resold in the future.

- **Collectibles and Digital Assets**: NFTs also have applications beyond digital art in **physical collectibles** such as **rare coins**, **vintage wine**, and even **sports**

memorabilia. NFTs linked to physical items can act as a **digital certificate** that guarantees the authenticity and ownership of these high-value assets.

- For example, a **vintage sports jersey** could be authenticated with an **NFT** tied to a blockchain record showing that it was owned by a specific athlete, providing provenance and helping to ensure the item is not a counterfeit.

3. Case Studies in Diamonds, Art, and Pharmaceuticals

- **Diamonds**: The diamond industry is notorious for **ethical sourcing issues** and the **lack of transparency** around the origins of diamonds. Blockchain is being used to provide full visibility into the diamond's journey, from the mine to the jeweler.
- **De Beers**, a major diamond company, has implemented a **blockchain system** to track diamonds from source to sale, ensuring that diamonds are conflict-free and ethically sourced. This also helps ensure that each diamond's **authenticity** and **value** are verifiable through an immutable ledger.
- **Art**: The art world, like luxury goods, faces significant problems with **forgery** and **fraud**. Blockchain can track the ownership history of art pieces, ensuring the **authenticity** and **provenance** of the work.
- **Verisart**, a company that provides **blockchain-based certificates of authenticity**, is working with artists, galleries, and collectors to track art pieces using blockchain. By assigning an **NFT** to each artwork, the **provenance** is recorded, and ownership can be easily transferred without the risk of fraud.

114

- **Pharmaceuticals**: Counterfeit drugs are a serious problem in the pharmaceutical industry, often leading to **safety risks** and **consumer harm**. Blockchain technology can provide a transparent record of a drug's journey through the supply chain, ensuring that it has not been tampered with and is safe for use.
- **MediLedger**, a blockchain network for the pharmaceutical industry, is working to improve the **traceability** and **authentication** of drugs, ensuring that patients receive legitimate medications and preventing counterfeit products from entering the market.

Summary

Blockchain is a powerful tool for ensuring the **provenance** and **authentication** of high-value and sensitive products, helping to combat fraud and guarantee quality. Key takeaways include:

- Blockchain allows for **authentication** of **luxury goods** by tracking their **provenance**, making it easy for consumers to verify their authenticity and ensuring product quality.
- **NFTs** provide a transparent, **immutable record** of **ownership** and **authenticity**, especially useful in the worlds of **art** and **collectibles**.
- **Case studies** in industries like **diamonds**, **art**, and **pharmaceuticals** show how blockchain is improving **traceability**, ensuring products are ethical, authentic, and safe.

By providing a **trustworthy ledger**, blockchain helps prevent **fraud**, ensures **authenticity**, and guarantees that valuable goods are what they claim to be—whether it's a **luxury handbag**, an **art masterpiece**, or a **medication**.

Smart Contracts for Supply Chain Automation

Smart contracts are one of the most transformative applications of **blockchain technology**. These self-executing contracts, where the terms and conditions are directly written into code, can automate processes across industries, particularly in **supply chain management**. When combined with blockchain, **smart contracts** offer enhanced transparency, security, and efficiency in everything from **payments** and **deliveries** to **inventory management** and **international trade**.

In this section, we will explore how **smart contracts** are being used to **automate supply chain processes**, streamline **international trade**, and drive **real-world** implementations in **companies** like **Walmart** and **Maersk**. We'll highlight the benefits these smart contracts bring, from **faster payments** and **automated inventory** to **reducing fraud** and improving **efficiency** in global trade.

1. Automating Processes like Payments, Deliveries, and Inventory Management

- **Automating Payments**: One of the key advantages of smart contracts in supply chain management is the ability to **automate payments**. When conditions specified in the contract are met—such as the delivery of goods or successful quality checks—the **payment is automatically triggered**.

- For example, a supplier ships goods to a retailer. Upon **delivery confirmation** (which could be tracked using IoT devices and blockchain), the **smart contract** automatically releases the payment, eliminating the need for manual approval and reducing administrative overhead.

- **Instant payments** can also be made across borders without delays due to bank processing times, offering a significant advantage in international trade.

- **Automating Deliveries**: Smart contracts can also automate **delivery processes**. The system can track goods as they move through the supply chain using blockchain, triggering actions when certain milestones are reached.

- For example, a **shipment** could be automatically released from customs once all required documentation (such as invoices, insurance, and health certifications) is verified on the blockchain. Once delivered, the smart contract could trigger a confirmation to both the supplier and buyer.

- **Inventory Management**: Smart contracts can help businesses track **inventory** in real-time, automatically updating stock levels as goods move through the supply chain.

- As items are sold or moved through the warehouse, **real-time updates** are made to the inventory records, which can then trigger automatic **restocking orders** when inventory levels fall below a certain threshold.

- This eliminates the need for manual intervention in tracking inventory, reducing the risk of human error and increasing supply chain efficiency.

2. Streamlining International Trade Using Blockchain

- **International Trade Efficiency**: Blockchain-based smart contracts streamline the complex process of **international trade** by reducing the need for intermediaries, speeding up the clearance process, and improving transparency. With a blockchain-based smart contract, trade partners can automate **key tasks** like customs clearance, documentation, and payment processing.
- For example, when a **shipment crosses borders**, the smart contract can ensure that all regulatory and legal requirements are met, verify that the necessary documents are in place, and automatically pay the relevant duties and taxes to customs authorities.
- This reduces the time it takes to clear goods through customs, which has traditionally been a major bottleneck in international trade, and also helps reduce the risk of fraud.
- **Cross-Border Payments**: In addition to simplifying physical logistics, blockchain can also automate **cross-border payments** using **cryptocurrencies** or **stablecoins**. These payments can be processed in real-time without the high fees and delays typically associated with international bank transfers, enhancing the efficiency of global trade.

3. Real-Life Implementations: Walmart, Maersk, and More

Several **global companies** have already implemented blockchain-based smart contracts to enhance their supply chain operations. Here are a few examples:

- **Walmart**: Walmart has partnered with **IBM** to develop a **blockchain-based system** for tracking food products in its supply chain. Using **smart contracts**, Walmart can quickly trace the journey of food products from farms to stores, verifying their **quality**, **safety**, and **authenticity**. This has been especially useful in the case of **food recalls**, where the time to identify the affected batches has been drastically reduced, improving food safety.
- For example, when an issue with a batch of spinach arose, Walmart was able to trace the source of contamination in **seconds** instead of the days or weeks it would have taken with traditional tracking methods.
- **Maersk**: **Maersk**, a global leader in shipping and logistics, has partnered with **IBM** to create **TradeLens**, a **blockchain-based platform** that facilitates the real-time tracking of cargo shipments. This platform uses smart contracts to automate tasks like **customs documentation**, **payments**, and **shipment tracking**, ensuring greater **transparency** and **efficiency**.
- Through **TradeLens**, all parties in the supply chain, including **shippers**, **customs authorities**, and **carriers**, have access to the same verified data in real-time, which reduces administrative costs and eliminates the need for paper-based processes.

- **Other Companies**: Many other organizations are also leveraging smart contracts for supply chain automation:
- **Nestlé**: Partnered with IBM to track the **coffee supply chain**, providing consumers with transparency about where their coffee comes from, how it was produced, and who produced it.
- **De Beers**: Uses blockchain to trace diamonds from mine to market, ensuring the **authenticity** and **ethical sourcing** of the diamonds they sell.
- **FedEx**: Has explored the use of blockchain for **automating logistics** and enhancing the transparency of its global supply chain.

Summary

In summary, **smart contracts** are revolutionizing supply chain management by automating critical processes like **payments**, **deliveries**, and **inventory management**, leading to greater **efficiency** and **cost savings**. These contracts are especially valuable for **international trade**, helping streamline **customs processes** and **cross-border payments**.

Key points include:

- **Smart contracts** automate processes in supply chain management, reducing the need for intermediaries and ensuring efficiency.
- **International trade** is becoming more streamlined through blockchain, reducing **delays** and **costs** associated with traditional trade procedures.
- Real-world examples like **Walmart** and **Maersk** show how blockchain-based smart contracts are already transform-

ing industries by improving **supply chain transparency**, **tracking**, and **automation**.

By automating tasks that were once manual and error-prone, blockchain-powered smart contracts can significantly reduce costs, improve efficiency, and build trust in the global supply chain.

3.3 Blockchain Beyond Cryptocurrency: Real-World Use Cases

Blockchain for Healthcare and Medical Records

The healthcare industry, with its vast amounts of **patient data** and **medical records**, presents a unique challenge in ensuring **privacy**, **security**, and **accuracy**. Traditional centralized systems for storing and managing medical data can be prone to errors, fraud, and breaches, with patients often having limited control over their own health information. Blockchain technology offers a **decentralized**, **secure**, and **transparent** solution to these problems by enabling **patient-centric data management**.

In this section, we will explore how **blockchain** can transform **healthcare data management**, protect **patient privacy**, and ensure **data accuracy**. We will also highlight **real-world examples** of blockchain-based **healthcare platforms** like **Medicalchain** and **Healthereum**, which are already helping to improve the security, **transparency**, and **efficiency** of medical record keeping.

1. Decentralized Healthcare Data Management for Patient Privacy

- **Patient-Centric Data Control**: One of the main benefits of blockchain in healthcare is its ability to give patients full control over their **medical data**. In a **decentralized system**, patient data is not stored in a single, central database, but across a **distributed ledger**. This means that instead of relying on a healthcare provider, patient, or insurance company to hold their records, individuals can have control over who accesses their information, how it's used, and for how long.

- With blockchain, **patients can grant access** to their records selectively and revoke permissions at any time. For example, if a patient visits a new healthcare provider, they can grant temporary access to their medical history for the duration of their consultation, while retaining full ownership of the data.

- **Privacy and Security**: The use of blockchain allows for **secure**, **encrypted** storage of sensitive patient information. Each transaction or update to a patient's record can be verified and logged in the blockchain, ensuring that the data remains tamper-proof and can only be accessed by authorized parties.

- **Cryptographic algorithms** encrypt patient data, ensuring it is secure even if the data is transmitted across multiple networks or accessed by multiple healthcare providers. This **privacy-first** approach is vital in ensuring that sensitive health information remains protected from breaches and unauthorized access.

2. Real-World Examples: Medicalchain and Healthereum

- **Medicalchain**: **Medicalchain** is a blockchain-based platform that allows patients to store their **medical records** on a decentralized ledger. This platform enables patients to have **full ownership** of their data while allowing healthcare professionals to access the information in real-time.
- The platform leverages blockchain's **immutability** to create a **secure digital record** of a patient's health history, which is easily accessible by both the patient and their healthcare providers. This eliminates the need for paper-based medical records, reduces administrative overhead, and allows for **faster and more accurate diagnoses**.
- Medicalchain's system also includes the use of **smart contracts** to facilitate secure transactions between healthcare providers and patients, ensuring that the terms of any treatment or consultation are transparent and automatically enforced.
- **Healthereum**: **Healthereum** is another blockchain-based healthcare platform that focuses on incentivizing **patient engagement** and ensuring **accurate medical records**. The platform uses **tokens** to reward patients for taking care of their health, such as attending appointments, undergoing tests, or following prescribed treatments. These **health tokens** are recorded on the blockchain, ensuring that patient actions are verified and tracked

transparently.

- The blockchain ledger ensures that the **data is accurate**, reducing the likelihood of fraudulent claims or inaccurate medical records. By encouraging patient participation in their own care, Healthereum enhances **patient engagement**, which can lead to better health outcomes.

3. Ensuring Data Accuracy and Preventing Fraud in Medical Records

- **Immutable and Transparent Records**: In traditional systems, medical records can be **altered** or **manipulated**, whether intentionally or by mistake, leading to errors or fraudulent activities. Blockchain provides a **tamper-proof record** by creating an immutable ledger of medical transactions. Once data is added to the blockchain, it cannot be changed or deleted, ensuring that patient records remain **accurate** and **reliable**.
- Every time a healthcare provider updates a patient's record, the change is logged with a **time stamp** and **digital signature**, making it easy to track who made the changes and when. This level of transparency can help identify any discrepancies or fraudulent activities, improving the **integrity** of medical records.
- **Preventing Fraud and Reducing Errors**: Blockchain's **decentralized** nature and cryptographic security prevent the unauthorized alteration or tampering of patient data. This is especially important in a healthcare environment where fraud, such as **false billing**, **identity theft**, or **unauthorized treatments**, can be a serious problem.
- By integrating blockchain into the healthcare system, the

industry can create a **secure audit trail** of all transactions and actions related to patient care. This ensures that both healthcare providers and patients can trust the accuracy and integrity of the medical information.

Summary

In summary, blockchain offers the healthcare industry a way to address critical issues like **data privacy**, **security**, and **accuracy** in medical records. Key points include:

- **Decentralized healthcare data management** empowers patients to control and share their medical records securely, ensuring **privacy** and **ownership** of personal health data.
- **Real-world examples** like **Medicalchain** and **Healthereum** demonstrate the practical application of blockchain in healthcare, improving access to medical records and incentivizing patient engagement.
- Blockchain's **immutable ledger** ensures that medical records are accurate, tamper-proof, and transparent, helping to **prevent fraud** and **reduce errors** in patient data.

By integrating blockchain technology into healthcare systems, the industry can provide more **secure**, **transparent**, and **patient-centered care**, improving both **data management** and **healthcare outcomes**.

Voting Systems and Blockchain Democracy

The idea of using blockchain to revolutionize **voting systems** and ensure **secure**, **transparent**, and **tamper-proof** elections has garnered increasing attention in recent years. Traditional voting systems, whether electronic or paper-based, are vulnerable to **fraud**, **errors**, and **manipulation**. Voter data can be altered, and election results can be disputed, which undermines public trust in the democratic process. Blockchain technology offers a potential solution by providing an **immutable, transparent, and decentralized** record of votes, ensuring **integrity** and **accountability** at every stage of the election process.

In this section, we will explore how blockchain can **ensure secure elections**, the **pilot projects** that have tested blockchain voting systems, and the **challenges** and **solutions** related to voter anonymity and scalability.

1. How Blockchain Can Ensure Secure, Transparent Elections

- **Decentralized and Tamper-Proof Voting Records**: Blockchain's core characteristic is its ability to create a **secure, decentralized ledger** that can record transactions (in this case, votes) in a way that cannot be altered after they have been recorded. Each vote would be encrypted and represented as a **block** in the blockchain, linked to previous blocks in the chain, forming a secure and permanent record.
- The **transparency** of blockchain means that each vote can be publicly verified by anyone, ensuring that the

election results cannot be manipulated or tampered with. If a candidate's vote tally changes, the blockchain ledger provides a transparent audit trail, allowing authorities to immediately detect any irregularities.

- The system ensures that each voter can only cast **one vote**. This eliminates the risk of **vote duplication**, **vote buying**, or **voter impersonation**. With **cryptographic validation**, voters can be sure that their vote is counted accurately and securely.

- **Real-Time Verification**: Blockchain can allow election officials to verify the status of votes in real-time. As votes are cast, the system can immediately confirm that they have been correctly recorded, **eliminating the need for manual counting** or reliance on centralized systems that could be susceptible to errors or tampering. This can also reduce the potential for human errors during the **vote tallying** process.

- **Transparency**: Since blockchain provides a **publicly accessible ledger**, election results can be tracked and verified at every stage. This can enhance **voter trust** by providing complete visibility into the election process, from registration to voting to final results. With the **blockchain's immutable ledger**, stakeholders can be sure that the results are a true and fair representation of the electorate's choices.

2. Pilot Projects and Blockchain-Based Voting Systems

Several **pilot projects** have tested blockchain-based voting systems, showing promising results in terms of **security**, **transparency**, and **efficiency**. Some of the most notable projects include:

- **Estonia's e-Residency and Blockchain Voting**: Estonia has been at the forefront of digital innovation and is known for its blockchain-based **e-Residency** program, which allows people from all over the world to access Estonian services and even vote in local elections. While **blockchain voting** is still being tested, Estonia's e-voting infrastructure already incorporates cryptographic security measures and digital identity verification, making it one of the most advanced examples of a **digital democracy**.
- **West Virginia, USA**: In 2018, **West Virginia** implemented a **blockchain-based voting system** for overseas military personnel during the midterm elections. Using **Voatz**, an app that runs on a blockchain network, West Virginia allowed military members to vote securely through their smartphones. The system used blockchain to **verify identities, secure votes**, and **ensure transparency**. Although this was a **pilot project**, it demonstrated the potential of using blockchain to allow for secure and remote voting in elections.
- **Sierra Leone**: In 2018, **Sierra Leone** conducted the first national election in Africa to use blockchain technology. The blockchain-based voting system was used for the election results tabulation process, helping to ensure the integrity of the vote count and reduce the chances of election fraud.

3. Overcoming Challenges: Voter Anonymity and Scalability

While blockchain offers significant advantages for voting systems, there are still some **key challenges** that need to be addressed:

- **Voter Anonymity**: One of the most important features of voting is **voter anonymity**, ensuring that individual votes cannot be traced back to the person who cast them. Blockchain can provide **anonymity** through **zero-knowledge proofs** or other encryption methods, allowing votes to be recorded on the blockchain while ensuring that no one can link a vote to a particular individual.
- To preserve anonymity, **privacy-focused blockchain systems** must be implemented, such as those that use advanced cryptography to mask voters' identities while still validating the legitimacy of their votes.
- **Scalability**: One of the challenges of using blockchain for voting is its ability to handle **large-scale elections**. **Blockchain networks** like **Bitcoin** and **Ethereum** have faced challenges in scaling to process a large number of transactions in a short amount of time. For elections that involve millions of voters, the **speed** and **cost** of processing votes must be addressed.
- **Layer 2 solutions** (such as **off-chain transactions** or **sidechains**) and more **efficient consensus algorithms** (like **Proof of Stake** instead of **Proof of Work**) could help to scale blockchain networks to handle the demands of national or global elections.
- **Accessibility and Adoption**: For blockchain voting to be

successful, voters need to have access to the necessary technology (smartphones or computers) and be comfortable using it. Ensuring that the system is **user-friendly** and accessible to people from all walks of life, including **the elderly** or **those with limited access to technology**, is a challenge that will need to be addressed to ensure **broad adoption**.

Summary

In summary, blockchain has the potential to revolutionize voting systems by offering a **secure**, **transparent**, and **tamper-proof** way to conduct elections. Key points include:

- **Secure, decentralized voting**: Blockchain ensures that each vote is counted accurately and cannot be altered after the fact, providing a transparent and trustworthy election process.
- **Pilot projects** like those in **Estonia**, **West Virginia**, and **Sierra Leone** have demonstrated the practical benefits of blockchain-based voting, but challenges related to **voter anonymity** and **scalability** remain.
- **Solutions** such as **zero-knowledge proofs** and **layer 2 technologies** may address these challenges, allowing blockchain to scale effectively and ensure **voter privacy**.

Blockchain-based voting systems can increase public trust in elections, provide better security, and streamline election processes, potentially transforming the way democracies operate worldwide.

Blockchain for Intellectual Property Protection

Intellectual property (IP) represents the creative and innovative works of individuals and organizations—whether they are **inventions**, **art**, **music**, **literature**, or **brands**. However, in today's digital age, IP faces significant challenges, such as **piracy**, **counterfeiting**, **unauthorized use**, and **difficulty in proving ownership**. Traditional systems of IP protection, such as registration with government agencies, can be slow, expensive, and prone to errors or disputes. This is where **blockchain technology** offers a transformative solution.

Blockchain can provide a **secure, transparent, and immutable record** of ownership and transactions related to intellectual property, which is vital for creators, inventors, and companies who want to protect their work and assert their rights. In this section, we will explore how blockchain can be used to **protect copyrights, patents, and trademarks**, how it can help **prevent piracy** in industries like **music**, **art**, and **film**, and some **real-world examples** of blockchain platforms like **Ascribe** and **Po.et** that are already leveraging this technology for IP protection.

1. Using Blockchain to Protect Copyrights, Patents, and Trademarks

- **Transparent and Immutable Ownership Records**: Blockchain technology provides an **immutable ledger** where every transaction or update to an intellectual property right (such as a copyright, patent, or trademark) is permanently recorded and can't be altered. This provides a **publicly verifiable record** of ownership and allows creators to **prove** their rights over their creations.

- For example, if an artist creates a digital painting, they can upload a **timestamped and encrypted record** of the artwork to the blockchain. This record serves as proof that the artist created the work at a specific time and holds **ownership** of the piece.

- Blockchain also allows creators to **register** their IP directly on the blockchain, ensuring that their ownership is **immediately recorded** without the need for expensive registration or intermediary processes. Additionally, by using blockchain's **cryptographic signatures**, creators can **prove ownership** without having to disclose their identity or location, thus maintaining their privacy.

- **Smart Contracts for Licensing and Royalties**: Smart contracts can be used to automate licensing agreements and manage **royalty payments**. These contracts can automatically execute predefined terms when certain conditions are met—such as when a piece of music is played or a digital artwork is purchased. This **automation** ensures that creators are paid fairly and promptly when their IP is used.

- For example, a musician can set up a **smart contract** that automatically distributes royalties every time their song is streamed on a platform, ensuring transparency and reducing the potential for disputes.

2. Preventing Content Piracy in the Music, Art, and Film Industries

- **Digital Provenance and Anti-Piracy**: Blockchain can help combat content piracy by creating a **transparent history of ownership** for digital content. In industries like **music**, **art**, and **film**, where piracy and unauthorized distribution are rampant, blockchain can provide a way to track the **origin** and **provenance** of digital files.

- Blockchain allows for the creation of a **digital certificate of authenticity** for digital content. Each time a digital file (such as a music track, video, or image) is transferred or sold, the transaction is recorded on the blockchain, making it easier to detect **unauthorized copies** or **counterfeit versions** of the content.

- For example, if a filmmaker releases a new film, the ownership of each **digital copy** can be tracked on the blockchain. This makes it much harder for pirates to distribute illegal copies without being detected, as the blockchain record will show the **original source** and **valid ownership** of each copy.

- **Global Distribution without Intermediaries**: Blockchain technology enables content creators to **distribute** their work **directly** to their audiences without relying on intermediaries like record labels, art galleries, or streaming services. This **peer-to-peer model** gives creators more control over how their work is used, shared, and monetized, reducing the risk of piracy or exploitation by third parties.

- By using **cryptocurrencies** for transactions and **blockchain-based platforms** for distribution, artists can sell their work directly to their fans and receive **instant payments**, while ensuring that they retain full rights over the content.

3. Examples of Blockchain IP Platforms: Ascribe and Po.et

- **Ascribe**: Ascribe is a **blockchain-based platform** that allows artists and creators to **register** and **protect** their digital artwork, music, and other creative works. The platform uses blockchain to **timestamp** and **authenticate** creative works, providing an **immutable record** of the creation and ownership of the work.

- **Artists** can use Ascribe to **track the provenance** of their digital works, allowing them to **prove ownership** and prevent unauthorized copies. Ascribe also allows creators to **license** their works, ensuring that they are compensated for their efforts. This has been especially valuable in the **art** and **digital content** industries, where piracy and counterfeiting are common.

- **Po.et**: Po.et is a **blockchain platform** for creators to **manage their intellectual property** rights for digital content such as articles, blogs, and other written works. Po.et uses blockchain to create a **public ledger** of digital media, providing a **proof of authorship** and a way to track the **usage** and **licensing** of content.

- Po.et allows creators to register their work on the platform, ensuring that they can prove ownership and **license** their content to others. It also allows for **monetization** of digital content by integrating with other platforms to enable the purchase and sale of creative works.

Summary

Blockchain technology offers numerous benefits for the protection and management of **intellectual property**. Key points include:

- Blockchain provides an **immutable and transparent ledger** for protecting **copyrights**, **patents**, and **trademarks**, allowing creators to prove ownership and manage their IP rights more efficiently.
- It helps prevent **piracy** and unauthorized distribution in the **music, art**, and **film industries** by creating **digital provenance** and allowing creators to track the ownership and distribution of their works.
- **Smart contracts** automate licensing and royalty payments, ensuring fair compensation for creators and reducing the potential for disputes.
- Platforms like **Ascribe** and **Po.et** demonstrate how blockchain is already being used to **protect** and **monetize** intellectual property in creative industries.

Blockchain is poised to transform the way we protect, manage, and distribute intellectual property, empowering creators and offering new opportunities for secure, transparent, and fair IP management.

Chapter 4: The Future of Blockchain and Cryptocurrencies

4.1 The Potential for Mass Adoption of Blockchain

How Blockchain Could Revolutionize Industries

Blockchain technology is often seen as a disruptor in the financial world, but its potential extends far beyond cryptocurrencies. The fundamental principles of **decentralization**, **security**, **transparency**, and **immutability** can be applied across virtually every industry, unlocking new efficiencies, simplifying complex processes, reducing costs, and increasing trust. In this section, we will explore how blockchain is poised to revolutionize sectors like **government**, **healthcare**, **logistics**, and **entertainment**, and examine how cross-industry collaborations are accelerating its adoption.

1. Potential Use Cases Across Sectors

- **Government**: Blockchain can improve **public sector services** by streamlining processes like **voter registration**, **land title management**, and **identity verification**. By replacing traditional, paper-based systems with blockchain, governments can eliminate inefficiencies, reduce corruption, and improve citizen access to services.

- For example, blockchain could create an immutable, transparent record of **voting** in elections, ensuring **fairness** and **security**. It could also be used for managing government services like **welfare distribution**, ensuring that funds are used correctly and reducing the potential for fraud.

- **Healthcare**: In healthcare, blockchain can provide **secure, decentralized management** of **patient records**. Blockchain could give patients full control over their data while ensuring that it remains **secure** and **accessible** to authorized parties like doctors, hospitals, and insurance providers. This could significantly reduce **data breaches** and **fraud** in medical records.

- Blockchain can also be used to track the **supply chain** of **pharmaceutical products**, ensuring that medicines are authentic and safe, and preventing the circulation of counterfeit drugs.

- Additionally, blockchain's role in **clinical trials** and **medical research** could streamline the tracking of results, improving transparency and reducing the potential for manipulation.

- **Logistics**: In industries like **shipping, transportation**, and **supply chain management**, blockchain can provide a secure, transparent, and automated way to track goods as they move through the supply chain. Blockchain enables **real-time tracking** of shipments, ensuring that parties involved in the supply chain (from manufacturers to retailers) can verify the status of goods at any point in the journey.

- **IBM and Maersk**'s collaboration on the **TradeLens** blockchain platform is a perfect example of how blockchain can streamline logistics. By tracking shipments on a blockchain, it allows for **faster**, **more accurate** transactions, reduces paperwork, and improves visibility for all parties involved in international trade.
- **Entertainment**: The **entertainment industry** can leverage blockchain for **digital rights management** (DRM) and **content distribution**. By creating immutable records of ownership and transactions, blockchain can help creators protect their **intellectual property** and reduce piracy. It can also simplify the **royalty distribution** process, ensuring that content creators, musicians, filmmakers, and other stakeholders are paid fairly and promptly for their work.
- Blockchain can facilitate **direct artist-to-fan interactions** without relying on intermediaries like record labels or streaming platforms, providing artists with more control over their earnings.

2. The Role of Blockchain in Simplifying Processes, Cutting Costs, and Increasing Transparency

Blockchain's most compelling value proposition across industries is its ability to simplify processes, reduce reliance on intermediaries, and enhance **transparency**.

- **Simplification of Complex Processes**: Blockchain enables businesses to automate and simplify processes by creating **smart contracts** that execute when predefined conditions are met. For example, in supply chains, smart contracts can automatically trigger payments when goods are delivered, reducing paperwork and the time it takes to process transactions.

- In the healthcare industry, smart contracts could automate the verification and payment processes for medical claims, eliminating administrative overhead and reducing fraud.

- **Cost Reduction**: Blockchain helps reduce the need for **middlemen** or intermediaries, thus lowering transaction costs. In the financial industry, for example, blockchain can facilitate **cross-border payments** without the need for banks or payment processors, reducing fees and speeding up transactions.

- In logistics, by eliminating paper-based documentation and reducing administrative costs, blockchain can streamline processes and improve operational efficiency, ultimately reducing costs across the supply chain.

- **Increasing Transparency**: One of the most significant advantages of blockchain is its ability to provide **transparency** in transactions. Every transaction is recorded on a public ledger, making it easily auditable and verifiable by anyone with access to the network. This transparency is especially beneficial in sectors like government, healthcare, and logistics, where accountability is crucial.

- For example, in the supply chain, all parties can access and verify the history of a product, from raw materials to final delivery, improving traceability and reducing the risk of fraud or counterfeit goods.

3. Exploring Cross-Industry Collaborations

Cross-industry collaborations are accelerating the implementation of blockchain solutions, and industries are increasingly recognizing the potential for blockchain to revolutionize not just their own sectors, but also the broader business ecosystem.

- **IBM and Maersk (TradeLens)**: The partnership between IBM and Maersk has created the **TradeLens** platform, a blockchain-based solution for managing global trade. This collaboration has enabled stakeholders across the supply chain—from suppliers to customs officials—to access the same data in real time, eliminating inefficiencies and improving transparency. The platform has the potential to streamline the shipping process by reducing the amount of paper-based documentation, speeding up clearance times, and reducing the risk of fraud.
- **Microsoft and Healthcare Providers**: Microsoft's **Azure Blockchain Service** is collaborating with various healthcare providers to streamline **patient data management**. The goal is to use blockchain to **secure patient records**, facilitate **cross-provider data sharing**, and ensure that healthcare providers have access to accurate, up-to-date information.
- Additionally, blockchain can help track **medical supply chains**, ensuring that pharmaceuticals are safe, counterfeit-free, and delivered in a timely manner.
- **Walmart and Blockchain in Food Safety**: Walmart is using blockchain technology to improve food safety by **tracking food products** from farm to shelf. This improves transparency in the food supply chain and helps

trace contaminated products quickly, reducing the time it takes to address potential public health risks. Walmart is working with **IBM** on the **Food Trust** blockchain platform to track the origin and journey of food items, ensuring food safety, freshness, and quality.

Summary

Blockchain technology is poised to revolutionize a wide range of industries, bringing significant benefits such as **improved efficiency**, **reduced costs**, **enhanced transparency**, and **automated processes**. Key takeaways include:

- **Government**, **healthcare**, **logistics**, and **entertainment** are just a few examples of sectors where blockchain is already showing its potential to improve existing processes.
- Blockchain simplifies complex processes, reduces costs by eliminating intermediaries, and enhances **transparency** by providing immutable, publicly accessible records.
- Cross-industry collaborations like **IBM and Maersk's TradeLens** and **Walmart's Food Trust** demonstrate how blockchain can bridge industries and create more efficient, secure systems across sectors.

As more industries adopt blockchain technology, we can expect to see widespread transformation, unlocking new opportunities, reducing inefficiencies, and enhancing trust in systems that were previously opaque or vulnerable to fraud.

Mainstream Adoption of Cryptocurrencies

Cryptocurrencies, once considered a niche investment, are increasingly making their way into the mainstream. From **traditional financial institutions** integrating **blockchain technology** to **central banks** exploring **digital currencies** (CBDCs), the financial landscape is undergoing a profound transformation. Alongside this, the role of **cryptocurrency in e-commerce** and **everyday transactions** is expanding, as more businesses and consumers recognize its benefits. This section will explore how **traditional finance** is adopting **blockchain** and **crypto**, the potential impact of **Central Bank Digital Currencies (CBDCs)**, and the growing **role of crypto** in **e-commerce** and **day-to-day purchases**.

1. How Traditional Finance Institutions Are Integrating Blockchain and Crypto

Traditional financial institutions, including banks, investment firms, and payment processors, have historically viewed cryptocurrencies with skepticism, largely due to their volatility and the lack of regulatory frameworks. However, the situation is changing rapidly as blockchain technology becomes recognized for its potential to improve efficiency, reduce costs, and streamline operations.

- **Banks and Financial Services**: Many banks are now adopting blockchain for its **speed** and **security** in processing cross-border payments. Blockchain can reduce the time and costs associated with international money transfers, which typically involve multiple intermediaries and take several days to process. By using blockchain, financial institutions can conduct **real-time settlement** of payments, significantly reducing costs and enhancing transparency.

- For instance, **JP Morgan** has launched its own **blockchain-based payment network** (Liink), which allows for faster, cheaper international money transfers between banks. Similarly, **Santander** and other major banks are investing in blockchain-based payment solutions.

- **Investment Firms and Wealth Management**: Institutional investment firms, such as **Grayscale** and **Fidelity**, are increasingly offering **cryptocurrency investment products**. These products give traditional investors exposure to digital assets like **Bitcoin** and **Ethereum**, making it easier for them to invest without needing to directly purchase or store cryptocurrencies. Investment firms are also using blockchain to enhance **trade settlement** and **clearing** processes, reducing the time and risk involved in executing financial transactions.

- **Payment Processors**: Companies like **PayPal** and **Visa** have taken significant steps to integrate cryptocurrency into mainstream payment systems. PayPal, for example, allows users to buy, sell, and hold cryptocurrencies like Bitcoin, Ethereum, and Litecoin directly within their accounts. **Visa** and **Mastercard** have also announced partnerships with crypto firms, enabling **crypto-to-fiat payment solutions**. These companies are helping make cryptocurrencies more accessible for everyday transactions, especially in digital wallets and e-commerce platforms.

2. Central Bank Digital Currencies (CBDCs) and Their Potential Impact

Central Bank Digital Currencies (CBDCs) represent an entirely new approach to digital money. Unlike decentralized cryptocurrencies like Bitcoin or Ethereum, CBDCs are issued and controlled by a central bank, meaning they are a **government-backed digital version of fiat currency**. Central banks around the world are increasingly exploring the possibility of issuing their own digital currencies, with some countries already launching or piloting CBDCs.

- **Why CBDCs Matter**: CBDCs could significantly alter the way we interact with money. By providing a **digital equivalent of physical cash**, CBDCs could offer greater **efficiency**, **security**, and **inclusivity**. For example, they could enable **real-time, low-cost cross-border payments**, reduce reliance on cash, and improve access to financial services for **unbanked populations**.
- **China's Digital Yuan** is one of the most prominent examples of a fully operational CBDC. The **People's Bank of China** has already started testing the digital yuan in major cities, aiming to reduce its dependency on the US dollar in global trade and create a more efficient payment system domestically.
- The **European Central Bank** and **Federal Reserve** are also exploring CBDCs, with the **digital euro** and **digital dollar** currently in the research and development phase. If successfully launched, CBDCs could challenge the role of cryptocurrencies like Bitcoin in global finance.
- **Impact on the Global Financial System**: CBDCs could

have significant implications for the global financial system. They could **reduce transaction costs**, **increase financial inclusion**, and provide central banks with more effective tools for **monetary policy**. By using CBDCs, central banks could directly manage **interest rates**, **inflation**, and **currency circulation** without relying on traditional banks or intermediaries. However, CBDCs also raise concerns about **privacy** and **government surveillance** of financial transactions, which could limit the anonymity traditionally associated with cash transactions.

3. The Role of Crypto in E-Commerce and Everyday Transactions

Cryptocurrency is no longer just an asset for investment or speculation; it is increasingly being used as a **medium of exchange** in **e-commerce** and **daily purchases**. As more companies and consumers adopt digital currencies, we are seeing the rise of **cryptocurrency-based payments**, from **online shopping** to **in-store purchases**.

- **E-Commerce and Retail**: Major online platforms such as **Amazon** and **eBay** are exploring ways to accept cryptocurrencies for payments. At the same time, smaller e-commerce platforms are already accepting Bitcoin, Ethereum, and other cryptocurrencies as payment for goods and services. Additionally, **payment processors** like **Coinbase Commerce** allow merchants to accept crypto payments easily and convert them into their preferred currency, providing businesses with the flexibility to accept digital currencies.

- For example, **Newegg**, an electronics retailer, accepts Bitcoin as payment for its products. **Overstock** and **Shopify** are also actively supporting cryptocurrency payments, making it easier for users to pay for everyday items using digital assets.

- **Physical Retail Stores**: Several physical stores are now accepting cryptocurrencies, particularly in tech-forward cities like **San Francisco**, **New York**, and **London**. Retailers like **Starbucks** (via **Bakkt**), **Whole Foods**, and **AT&T** have started accepting Bitcoin and other cryptocurrencies through third-party payment processors.

- With cryptocurrency payments becoming more seamless through services like **Apple Pay** and **Google Pay**, which are integrating crypto payment solutions, we are likely to see broader adoption in brick-and-mortar retail spaces in the future.

- **Benefits for Consumers and Merchants**: The use of cryptocurrency in e-commerce and everyday transactions offers numerous benefits. For **consumers**, it provides an alternative payment method that can be more **secure** and **private** than traditional banking or credit card payments. It also reduces the need for intermediaries, enabling **peer-to-peer transactions** without the high fees associated with credit card processing.

- For **merchants**, accepting cryptocurrencies can help **expand their customer base**, particularly in regions where people have limited access to traditional banking services. Cryptocurrencies also allow businesses to avoid **chargebacks** and fraud, as crypto transactions are **irre-**

versible once confirmed.

Summary

The mainstream adoption of cryptocurrencies is rapidly accelerating across multiple sectors, including **traditional finance**, **central banking**, and **e-commerce**. Key takeaways include:

- **Financial institutions** are integrating blockchain and cryptocurrency into their operations to improve **payment processing**, reduce costs, and offer new investment opportunities.
- **Central Bank Digital Currencies (CBDCs)** are being explored by governments as a way to offer **digital currency alternatives** that are government-backed and could reshape monetary systems.
- **Cryptocurrencies** are increasingly accepted in **e-commerce** and **physical retail**, providing both consumers and merchants with **faster**, **cheaper**, and more **secure** alternatives to traditional payment methods.

As cryptocurrencies become a more integrated part of the global economy, we are likely to see further innovations and increasing adoption across industries and in daily life.

Challenges to Mass Adoption

While the potential of blockchain technology and cryptocurrencies is immense, there are still significant **challenges** that hinder their **mass adoption**. These challenges range from **technical barriers** such as **scalability** and **energy**

consumption, to **regulatory hurdles** concerning **taxation**, **compliance**, and **security**, as well as **public perception** issues related to **trust** in decentralized technologies. In this section, we will explore these obstacles in detail and how they impact the widespread adoption of blockchain and cryptocurrencies.

1. Technical Barriers: Scalability, Speed, and Energy Consumption

One of the primary obstacles to mass adoption is the **technical limitations** of blockchain technology itself. Despite its groundbreaking nature, the current infrastructure of many blockchain networks, particularly **Bitcoin** and **Ethereum**, faces significant challenges in terms of **scalability** and **speed**.

- **Scalability**: Blockchain networks are designed to be secure and decentralized, but this often comes at the cost of performance. Most public blockchains struggle to handle a large volume of transactions at once. For example, Bitcoin can handle roughly 7 **transactions per second** (TPS), while Ethereum can process about **30 TPS**, which is far less than traditional payment systems like **Visa**, which can process tens of thousands of transactions per second.

- This scalability issue limits the capacity of blockchain networks to handle the **global transaction volume** required for mass adoption. For blockchain to become a mainstream payment system, it needs to scale to meet the demands of millions of users worldwide.

- **Transaction Speed**: In addition to scalability, **transaction speed** is another concern. Blockchain transactions require validation and consensus, which can take time.

While some blockchain networks like **Solana** and **Polygon** are working on solutions to increase speed, many blockchains still face delays, making them less attractive for real-time or high-volume transactions.

- **Energy Consumption**: The energy consumption of blockchain networks, particularly those using **Proof of Work (PoW)** consensus mechanisms like Bitcoin, is another major hurdle. **Bitcoin mining** consumes vast amounts of electricity due to the high computational power required for miners to solve cryptographic puzzles. This has led to concerns about the environmental impact of cryptocurrency mining.

- While Ethereum has transitioned to a more energy-efficient **Proof of Stake (PoS)** model, other blockchains are still grappling with the environmental costs of running decentralized networks.

2. Regulatory and Legal Hurdles: Taxation, Compliance, and Security

The legal and regulatory landscape surrounding cryptocurrencies is still evolving, and many governments are struggling to determine how to classify, regulate, and tax cryptocurrencies.

- **Taxation**: One of the biggest challenges for mass adoption is the unclear or inconsistent approach to cryptocurrency **taxation**. In many jurisdictions, cryptocurrencies are treated as **assets** (like property or stocks) rather than as currency, which creates confusion for taxpayers and businesses alike. For example, in the U.S., the **IRS** taxes cryptocurrency transactions as capital gains, which can be burdensome for users and merchants who need to keep track of every transaction and calculate taxes accordingly.

- Inconsistent taxation policies across countries make it difficult for businesses to adopt cryptocurrencies and for users to understand their obligations. Governments need to establish clear, consistent regulations on cryptocurrency taxation to ensure compliance and provide clarity for users.

- **Compliance**: Compliance with existing financial regulations, including **Know Your Customer (KYC)** and **Anti-Money Laundering (AML)** requirements, is another major hurdle. Cryptocurrency exchanges and wallets are under increasing scrutiny to ensure that they are not being used for illicit activities. While the decentralized nature of blockchain is one of its defining features, it also complicates regulatory oversight and raises concerns about **money laundering** and **terrorist financing**.

- For cryptocurrencies to gain widespread acceptance, regulatory frameworks need to be developed that balance **decentralization** with the need for **compliance** to prevent misuse.

- **Security**: Cryptocurrencies and blockchain networks are not immune to security breaches. Hacks, scams, and vulnerabilities in smart contracts and exchanges have led to billions of dollars in losses. High-profile hacks, such as the **Mt. Gox** exchange collapse and the **DAO hack** on Ethereum, highlight the risks associated with the security of decentralized platforms.

- Ensuring the security of blockchain networks, exchanges, and smart contracts is crucial for building trust in the technology. This includes not only **technological solutions** but also ensuring proper **cybersecurity protocols** are in place.

3. Public Perception and Trust in Decentralized Technologies

Public perception and trust are often cited as significant barriers to the **widespread adoption of cryptocurrencies**. Although blockchain and cryptocurrencies offer numerous benefits, they are still viewed with **skepticism** by many, particularly in the mainstream.

- **Volatility**: One of the main concerns with cryptocurrencies is their **price volatility**. The extreme price swings seen in Bitcoin, Ethereum, and other cryptocurrencies can make them seem like speculative assets rather than stable forms of payment or investment. For mass adoption to occur, cryptocurrencies need to become more **stable** and **predictable** in value.
- The volatility also makes it harder for businesses to adopt cryptocurrency as a form of payment, as they may face unpredictable changes in the value of their revenues.
- **Lack of Understanding**: Many people still don't fully understand how blockchain and cryptocurrencies work. The **technical complexity** and **perceived risk** of using cryptocurrencies can be intimidating for individuals who are not familiar with the technology. **Financial literacy** and **education** on how cryptocurrencies function, how to use wallets, and how to stay secure are essential for overcoming this barrier.
- Without clear education and greater transparency, people

may avoid adopting blockchain and crypto due to fear or misunderstanding.

- **Trust in Decentralization**: Finally, there is the issue of **trust** in the **decentralized nature** of cryptocurrencies. Traditional financial systems are generally seen as trustworthy, with governments, banks, and financial institutions backing them. In contrast, cryptocurrencies are often seen as **unregulated**, **risky**, and **anonymous**, which can deter people from adopting them.
- However, the increasing integration of cryptocurrencies into **mainstream finance** (e.g., PayPal, Visa, banks) and the development of **centralized exchanges** and **stablecoins** is helping to bridge the trust gap.

Summary

While the potential for blockchain and cryptocurrencies is enormous, there are significant challenges that need to be addressed for mass adoption to occur. Key challenges include:

- **Technical barriers** such as **scalability**, **speed**, and **energy consumption**.
- **Regulatory hurdles** related to **taxation, compliance**, and **security**.
- **Public perception** issues stemming from **volatility, lack of understanding**, and **trust in decentralized systems**.

To realize the full potential of blockchain and cryptocurrencies, these obstacles must be overcome through **innovation, clear regulations**, and **public education**.

4.2 The Role of Regulation and Government in Crypto's Future

Global Regulatory Landscape

As the adoption of cryptocurrencies continues to grow, governments and regulatory bodies around the world are grappling with how to approach and regulate this new and disruptive technology. **Cryptocurrency regulation** is a highly complex and rapidly evolving area, with each country taking its own stance based on political, economic, and cultural factors. Some countries have embraced digital currencies, while others have imposed stringent regulations or outright bans. In this section, we will explore how different regions are responding to cryptocurrency regulation, examine specific case studies, and discuss the potential for **international collaboration** in establishing unified regulatory standards.

1. How Countries Are Responding to Cryptocurrency Regulation

The regulatory response to cryptocurrencies varies significantly from one country to another, depending on local economic conditions, technological adoption rates, and concerns about risks such as money laundering, tax evasion, and financial stability.

- **Supportive Stance**: Some countries are taking a **progressive** and **supportive approach**, seeking to integrate blockchain and cryptocurrencies into their financial systems. These countries aim to capitalize on the potential

153

of digital currencies and blockchain technology while establishing clear legal frameworks to ensure consumer protection and financial stability.

- **Examples**: **Switzerland**, **Singapore**, and **Malta** are known for their crypto-friendly regulatory environments. In **Switzerland**, for instance, **Zug** (also known as "Crypto Valley") is home to many blockchain startups and offers a supportive regulatory framework for crypto businesses. **Singapore** has established comprehensive rules for cryptocurrency exchanges, Initial Coin Offerings (ICOs), and Anti-Money Laundering (AML) compliance. **Malta** has enacted the **Virtual Financial Assets Act** to regulate digital assets, making it a hub for blockchain projects.

- **Restrictive Stance**: On the opposite end of the spectrum, several countries have taken a **restrictive approach**, seeking to limit the use of cryptocurrencies or outright banning them. These countries often cite concerns about **fraud**, **tax evasion**, **capital flight**, and the potential for digital currencies to undermine **monetary control**.

- **Examples**: **China** has implemented a **comprehensive ban** on cryptocurrency trading, mining, and Initial Coin Offerings (ICOs) in recent years. The Chinese government's crackdown on crypto is driven by concerns over financial stability and the use of digital currencies for illicit activities. Similarly, **India** has seen fluctuating regulatory responses, with the **Reserve Bank of India (RBI)** previously imposing banking restrictions on cryptocurrency businesses, though the **Supreme Court** lifted the ban in 2020.

- **Wait-and-See Approach**: Many countries, especially emerging markets, are adopting a **wait-and-see** approach, monitoring developments in the cryptocurrency space while gradually introducing regulations. These countries often recognize the potential benefits of blockchain technology but are cautious about rushing into regulation without fully understanding the implications.

- **Examples**: **Brazil** and **Mexico** are still exploring how to regulate cryptocurrencies. Both countries have been discussing the creation of frameworks for crypto taxation and anti-money laundering practices, though comprehensive regulation is still in development.

2. Case Studies: China's Ban, the U.S. SEC's Stance, and Europe's MiCA Regulations

- **China's Ban**: China has had one of the most stringent regulatory approaches toward cryptocurrencies. The government has banned cryptocurrency exchanges, ICOs, and mining operations, citing concerns over financial stability and capital outflows. While China's official stance on cryptocurrencies is negative, the country has simultaneously been at the forefront of **Central Bank Digital Currency (CBDC)** development with the **digital yuan**.

- Despite the ban on cryptocurrencies, China has continued to promote **blockchain technology** for use in various sectors, such as supply chain management and government services. The Chinese government has emphasized the importance of **centralized** digital currencies, which it can fully control, as opposed to decentralized assets like Bitcoin.

- **U.S. SEC's Stance**: The **U.S. Securities and Exchange**

Commission (SEC) has played a key role in regulating cryptocurrencies in the United States, particularly with respect to Initial Coin Offerings (ICOs) and **securities laws**. The SEC has taken a cautious approach, asserting that many cryptocurrencies may qualify as **securities** under U.S. law, which would subject them to strict regulatory oversight.

- The SEC's stance has been to apply existing securities regulations to the cryptocurrency space, particularly around the **Howey Test**, which determines whether an asset is a security based on its investment characteristics. This has led to several high-profile enforcement actions against crypto projects accused of selling unregistered securities.

- However, the SEC's approach has been criticized for its lack of clear guidelines, leading to uncertainty and confusion in the market. Some lawmakers are pushing for clearer cryptocurrency regulations, and the SEC continues to grapple with how to regulate digital assets in a rapidly evolving environment.

- **Europe's MiCA Regulations**: The **Markets in Crypto-Assets (MiCA)** regulation is one of the first comprehensive sets of regulations aimed at regulating cryptocurrencies in the **European Union**. MiCA is designed to provide a legal framework for crypto markets, protect consumers, and ensure the stability of the financial system.

- The MiCA regulation is set to cover a wide range of crypto-related activities, including **stablecoins**, **crypto exchanges**, **wallet providers**, and **ICO issuers**. It aims to create a single regulatory framework for the EU, allowing businesses to operate across member states with a harmonized approach to crypto regulation.

- One of the key provisions of MiCA is that it will introduce a licensing regime for crypto-asset service providers (CASPs), requiring them to adhere to strict **consumer protection** and **AML/KYC** requirements. MiCA is seen as an attempt to balance **innovation** with **consumer protection** and could serve as a model for other jurisdictions to follow.

3. The Potential for International Collaboration and Standards

While the regulatory landscape for cryptocurrencies is fragmented, there is a growing recognition that **international collaboration** is necessary to create a cohesive framework for the global crypto market. Several organizations are working toward creating **global standards** for cryptocurrency regulation.

- **The Financial Action Task Force (FATF)**: The **FATF**, an international organization that sets global standards for combating money laundering and terrorist financing, has issued guidance on how cryptocurrency exchanges and service providers should comply with **AML** and **KYC** requirements. While FATF's guidelines are not legally binding, they influence national regulations and encourage countries to align their regulatory frameworks.
- FATF has recommended that countries require cryptocurrency businesses to report suspicious activity and share customer information across borders, in line with traditional financial services. This is part of an effort to **reduce fraud** and **illicit activities** in the crypto space

while allowing legitimate businesses to thrive.

- **Global Consensus**: Achieving global consensus on cryptocurrency regulation remains challenging due to varying political, economic, and cultural factors. However, there is growing recognition that **harmonized standards** could help reduce the risks associated with cryptocurrencies, encourage innovation, and provide more certainty to businesses and investors.

- Countries may eventually adopt **international agreements** that balance **national sovereignty** with the need for **global cooperation** in regulating digital assets. Such efforts could foster greater confidence in the crypto ecosystem and allow cryptocurrencies to flourish within a well-defined legal and regulatory framework.

Summary

The **global regulatory landscape** for cryptocurrencies is complex and rapidly evolving. Key takeaways include:

- Different countries have adopted **varying approaches** to cryptocurrency regulation, ranging from **supportive** and **crypto-friendly** frameworks (e.g., Switzerland, Singapore) to **restrictive** or **banning** approaches (e.g., China).
- Specific case studies, such as **China's ban**, the **U.S. SEC's approach**, and the European **MiCA regulations**, show the diverse ways in which governments are attempting to regulate the cryptocurrency market.
- **International collaboration** and the creation of **global standards** could help reduce regulatory fragmentation and promote more consistent, transparent, and secure

cryptocurrency markets worldwide.

The Impact of Regulation on Blockchain and Crypto Innovation

As the cryptocurrency and blockchain industries continue to evolve, the role of **regulation** becomes increasingly significant. On one hand, **clear and fair regulations** can provide the foundation for a **secure and trustworthy environment** that promotes innovation and attracts investment. On the other hand, overly restrictive or unclear regulations can stifle creativity, hinder growth, and create uncertainty. In this section, we explore the delicate balance between **innovation** and **consumer protection** in the blockchain and crypto spaces, examining how regulation can either support or hinder industry growth, with examples from countries that have created **favorable regulatory environments**.

1. Balancing Innovation with Consumer Protection

One of the key challenges of regulating the blockchain and cryptocurrency space is finding the right balance between **encouraging innovation** and **ensuring consumer protection**.

- **Innovation:** The blockchain industry is still in its early stages, and there is tremendous potential for technological advances, new use cases, and business models. Regulation that is too restrictive can stifle this innovation by limiting the ability of companies to experiment and grow.
- **Consumer Protection:** At the same time, the industry is still relatively new and evolving, with significant risks

such as fraud, hacking, market manipulation, and investor loss. Regulatory frameworks can help protect consumers from these risks, ensuring transparency, security, and fair market practices.

- The key is to **create regulations that safeguard consumers** while **fostering growth** and **encouraging innovation**. Countries that get this balance right tend to be the most successful in attracting blockchain and crypto businesses.

2. How Regulation Can Enable or Hinder Growth

Regulation can have both positive and negative effects on the growth of the blockchain and cryptocurrency sectors, depending on how it is implemented.

- **Enabling Growth**: Well-crafted regulations can help build **trust** and **stability**, making it easier for investors, businesses, and consumers to participate in the crypto space. By creating a **clear legal framework**, regulations can lower the barriers to entry, encourage investment, and drive **mainstream adoption**.
- Example: **Switzerland** is often cited as a model for blockchain-friendly regulation. The Swiss government has developed a **clear regulatory framework** that covers **cryptocurrency trading**, **taxation**, **money laundering**, and **security concerns**. This has made Switzerland a hub for crypto startups and blockchain companies, with the country offering a **stable** and **predictable regulatory environment** that fosters growth and innovation.
- **Hindering Growth**: On the other hand, poorly designed

or overly stringent regulations can discourage investment and innovation, or even push companies to relocate to jurisdictions with more favorable rules. Excessive compliance costs, burdensome reporting requirements, or unclear legal frameworks can create barriers to entry, particularly for smaller companies or startups.

- Example: **China's restrictive policies**, including bans on cryptocurrency exchanges and initial coin offerings (ICOs), have stifled innovation in the country, forcing blockchain and crypto companies to relocate to more crypto-friendly regions. While China has continued to invest heavily in blockchain technology, its stance on cryptocurrencies has created uncertainty and limited growth opportunities in the sector.

3. Examples of Countries with Favorable Regulatory Environments

Some countries have recognized the potential of blockchain and cryptocurrencies and have created **regulatory environments** that encourage growth and innovation while ensuring adequate consumer protection. These countries often strike a balance between regulation and the need for a vibrant, innovative ecosystem.

- **Switzerland**: Switzerland is often considered the **leading example** of a crypto-friendly country with clear, supportive regulations. The Swiss government has embraced blockchain technology and has created a **legal framework** for cryptocurrencies and Initial Coin Offerings (ICOs). Swiss law provides clarity on how cryptocurrencies should be treated for tax purposes and covers the legal use of smart contracts. The country's **Crypto Valley** in Zug has become a hub for crypto startups, attracting global talent and investment.

- **Singapore**: Singapore has become a **global leader** in blockchain and crypto innovation, offering one of the most **progressive** and **transparent regulatory environments** in the world. The **Monetary Authority of Singapore (MAS)** has issued clear guidelines for crypto businesses and is actively working to **support innovation** in the financial technology space. Singapore's open stance on blockchain technology has attracted **numerous blockchain startups**, exchanges, and ICOs, making it one of the most vibrant crypto ecosystems in Asia.

- **Malta**: Malta has developed a comprehensive set of regulations for **cryptocurrency exchanges**, **ICOs**, and **distributed ledger technology (DLT)** companies. The **Malta Financial Services Authority (MFSA)** regulates the crypto sector, providing businesses with clear guidance on legal requirements and compliance. Malta has positioned itself as a **blockchain island**, attracting international companies and providing a supportive environment for crypto and blockchain-related activities.

4. The Risks of Over-Regulation and Under-Regulation

- **Over-Regulation**: When regulation is overly strict or complex, it can discourage innovation, delay the development of new blockchain-based projects, and drive businesses out of the country. Excessive regulatory burdens can also increase costs for companies, particularly smaller startups with fewer resources to navigate complex legal requirements. **Over-regulation** can potentially cause a **brain drain** in the crypto industry, where entrepreneurs and developers move to more **crypto-friendly** jurisdictions.

- **Under-Regulation**: On the other hand, **under-regulation** or the lack of any regulation can create an environment where **fraud**, **scams**, and **market manipulation** flourish. Without a clear legal framework, investors may face increased risks, and the industry as a whole may struggle to gain **mainstream adoption** and **institutional confidence**. For instance, when certain markets had minimal or no regulation for ICOs, many investors faced substantial losses due to fraudulent projects or pump-and-dump schemes.

Summary

The **impact of regulation** on blockchain and cryptocurrency innovation is profound. The right balance between consumer protection and fostering innovation is critical to the sector's growth. Clear and fair regulations can provide the stability needed for long-term development, while overly restrictive policies can stifle innovation and push companies out of the country.

- **Regulation can enable growth** by providing a clear framework that promotes investment, enhances trust, and ensures consumer protection.
- **Over-regulation** can hinder growth by creating unnecessary barriers and uncertainty, while **under-regulation**

can lead to fraud and instability.

- **Examples from Switzerland, Singapore, and Malta** demonstrate how favorable regulatory environments can create thriving blockchain ecosystems.

The Future of ICOs and Tokenization

The world of **Initial Coin Offerings (ICOs)** has evolved rapidly over the past few years, with new models such as **Security Token Offerings (STOs)** emerging as the future of fundraising in the blockchain space. ICOs, which initially allowed companies to raise capital by issuing new tokens to investors, faced significant challenges, including regulatory scrutiny, fraud, and volatility. As a result, STOs and other **tokenization** initiatives have begun to take center stage, providing a more **regulated**, **secure**, and **compliant** approach to digital fundraising and asset management.

In this section, we explore the **evolution of ICOs** into **STOs**, the legal considerations surrounding **tokenization**, and the **potential of tokenized real estate, art, and commodities**.

1. How ICOs Are Evolving into STOs

Initial Coin Offerings (ICOs) were a popular method for blockchain startups to raise funds by selling their native tokens to investors, typically without much regulatory oversight. While ICOs allowed for rapid fundraising, they also attracted criticism for being risky, often lacking transparency, and sometimes leading to fraudulent activities. This prompted regulators to step in and demand more accountability, leading to the emergence of a more **regulated** model known as **Security Token Offerings (STOs)**.

- **STOs** represent a **regulated approach** to tokenized fundraising, where tokens are issued as **securities**. These tokens are subject to the same legal requirements as traditional financial securities, ensuring that companies comply with **securities laws** and providing investors with greater protection.
- **STOs** offer increased **transparency**, **compliance**, and **investor protection** compared to ICOs. They are typically issued on **blockchain networks** that follow established regulatory frameworks, such as the **U.S. SEC's** (Securities and Exchange Commission) guidelines for tokenized securities.

As STOs grow in popularity, they are expected to **replace ICOs** as the primary method for raising funds in the blockchain industry, especially for **asset-backed** and **compliant projects**.

2. Legal Considerations in Tokenizing Assets and Securities

The tokenization of **assets** and **securities** involves converting real-world assets into **digital tokens** that can be bought, sold, and traded on the blockchain. This process opens up new opportunities for investing in traditionally illiquid assets such as real estate, art, and commodities. However, there are significant **legal considerations** that companies must navigate in this space:

- **Securities Regulation**: When assets are tokenized and sold to investors, they may be classified as **securities**. This means they must comply with regulations that govern **securities trading**, such as the **Securities Act of 1933** in the U.S. or similar laws in other countries. Tokenized assets that qualify as securities must follow strict rules regarding registration, disclosure, and investor protection.

- **Legal Frameworks**: Different countries have varying laws regarding the tokenization of assets. In some jurisdictions, **security token offerings (STOs)** are subject to **securities regulations**, while in others, tokenized assets may be regulated under **commodity or property laws**. It is essential for companies to understand the legal landscape in their jurisdiction before proceeding with tokenization.

- **Smart Contracts and Legal Validity**: The use of **smart contracts** to automate token transactions adds another layer of complexity. The smart contract must be legally valid and enforceable, which means it must be designed with proper legal documentation and **contractual terms**. Some jurisdictions are working to develop legal frameworks that recognize **smart contracts** as valid forms of agreement, while others are still working out the details.

3. The Potential of Tokenized Real Estate, Art, and Commodities

Tokenization is transforming the way we think about ownership and investment in a variety of asset classes. By converting physical assets into digital tokens, blockchain enables **fractional ownership** and the **liquidation of traditionally illiquid assets**. Here are some key areas where tokenization is expected to have a major impact:

- **Tokenized Real Estate**: The real estate market is one of the most exciting areas for tokenization. Real estate is typically a **highly illiquid** asset, and purchasing property can require significant capital. Tokenization allows **fractional ownership**, enabling individuals to invest in **real estate assets** with as little as a few hundred dollars. This could open up real estate investing to a broader audience, allowing for more **diverse portfolios** and **global access** to prime real estate markets.
- Example: Platforms like **RealT** and **Harbor** are already tokenizing real estate properties, offering fractionalized ownership of residential and commercial real estate through blockchain-based tokens.
- **Tokenized Art**: The art world has long been seen as a **luxury market** reserved for wealthy investors. Tokenizing art can enable **fractional ownership** of high-value pieces, allowing individuals to invest in artworks without needing to purchase the entire piece. Tokenization can also provide a **transparent** and **secure** record of ownership, making it easier to buy, sell, and track art on the blockchain.
- Example: **Maecenas** is a platform that allows users to

invest in tokenized artwork, giving access to **high-value art** without the need for large capital outlay.

- **Tokenized Commodities**: Commodities like **gold**, **oil**, and **agriculture** are already highly liquid, but tokenization offers a way to increase **transparency** and **liquidity** in the market. Investors can own and trade **fractionalized ownership** of physical commodities through digital tokens. This could democratize access to commodities and reduce the need for middlemen in the market.
- Example: **Swiss Gold** has created a platform where users can own **fractionalized gold tokens** backed by physical gold stored in vaults.

Summary

The future of ICOs and tokenization is moving toward **regulated, secure, and compliant fundraising models**. As ICOs evolve into **Security Token Offerings (STOs)**, they provide a more secure and trustworthy method for tokenizing assets and securities. Legal considerations, such as securities regulations and the use of smart contracts, must be addressed for successful tokenization. The potential for tokenizing **real estate**, **art**, and **commodities** offers new opportunities for fractional ownership, liquidity, and access to traditionally illiquid markets.

4.3 The Road Ahead: What to Expect in the Next Decade

Technological Innovations and Emerging Trends

As blockchain technology matures and adoption accelerates, we are witnessing the emergence of several **innovations and trends** that have the potential to shape the future of the industry. From **Layer 2 solutions** designed to enhance scalability, to the potential disruption posed by **quantum computing**, and the growing need for **interoperability** between different blockchain networks, these advancements are setting the stage for the next phase of blockchain evolution.

In this section, we'll explore the key technological innovations and emerging trends in the blockchain space, highlighting how each of these developments is paving the way for a more **efficient**, **secure**, and **interconnected** blockchain ecosystem.

1. The Rise of Layer 2 Solutions for Scaling

Blockchain scalability has been one of the most significant challenges facing the industry. As more users and transactions flood the networks, blockchains like Bitcoin and Ethereum can experience **congestion**, leading to higher transaction fees and slower confirmation times. **Layer 2 solutions** aim to solve these problems by operating on top of existing blockchains, increasing transaction throughput without compromising the **security** or **decentralization** of the underlying Layer 1 chain.

- **Lightning Network (Bitcoin)**: The Lightning Network is one of the most well-known Layer 2 solutions for Bitcoin. It enables faster and cheaper transactions by creating a secondary network where transactions can be conducted off-chain and only settled on the main Bitcoin blockchain when necessary. This significantly increases Bitcoin's **transaction speed** and reduces costs, making it more suitable for everyday transactions.

- **Polygon (Ethereum)**: Polygon is another prominent Layer 2 solution, designed to improve the scalability of the Ethereum blockchain. Polygon works by creating sidechains that can process transactions more efficiently than the Ethereum mainnet. These sidechains can handle **high transaction volumes** and are integrated with Ethereum, allowing assets and data to be transferred between them seamlessly.
- **Benefits of Layer 2 Solutions**:
- **Increased scalability** and **transaction speed**
- **Lower fees** for users and businesses
- **Improved user experience** for decentralized applications (dApps)

As Layer 2 solutions continue to evolve, they are expected to unlock new possibilities for **mass adoption** of blockchain technology, enabling high-volume use cases like **microtransactions**, **gaming**, and **payments**.

2. Quantum Computing's Potential Impact on Blockchain Technology

Quantum computing is a **revolutionary** field of computing that leverages the principles of **quantum mechanics** to perform calculations at speeds far beyond what is possible with traditional computers. While still in its infancy, quantum computing holds significant implications for blockchain technology, particularly in terms of **security**.

- **Quantum Threat to Cryptography**: Blockchain networks rely heavily on **cryptographic algorithms** (such as **RSA** and **Elliptic Curve Digital Signature Algorithm** or **ECDSA**) to secure transactions and maintain the integrity of the blockchain. Quantum computers have the potential to **break these cryptographic systems** by solving problems that classical computers would take millennia to crack.

- **Quantum-Resistant Blockchains**: In response to this potential threat, researchers are developing **quantum-resistant algorithms** that are designed to be secure even against the power of quantum computers. This includes **lattice-based cryptography** and **hash-based signatures**.

- **Future Impact**: While quantum computers are not yet advanced enough to break existing blockchain systems, the industry is already exploring ways to prepare for this future. The rise of **quantum computing** could force blockchain networks to upgrade their cryptographic standards, which will require significant innovation in **security protocols**.

3. Interoperability Between Different Blockchain Networks

Another key challenge facing blockchain technology today is the **lack of interoperability** between different blockchains. Currently, many blockchains operate in isolation, each with its own set of rules, governance, and asset standards. This creates a fragmented ecosystem where data and assets are siloed, preventing seamless interaction across platforms.

- **Interoperability Solutions**: To address this issue, various projects are working on **cross-chain** solutions that enable different blockchains to communicate and exchange value with each other. These solutions could enable users and businesses to move assets between blockchains in a secure and efficient way, unlocking new use cases for decentralized finance (DeFi), supply chain tracking, and more.
- **Polkadot**: Polkadot is a blockchain platform designed specifically for **interoperability**. It connects multiple blockchains, known as **parachains**, allowing them to communicate and share information securely. Polkadot's **relay chain** acts as the central hub, ensuring that all connected blockchains can interact with one another.
- **Cosmos**: Another key project in the interoperability space is **Cosmos**, which aims to create an **internet of blockchains** by allowing multiple blockchains to transfer data and value seamlessly using the **Inter-Blockchain Communication (IBC) protocol**.
- **Benefits of Interoperability**:
- **Cross-chain DeFi** applications
- **Unified** blockchain ecosystem
- **Frictionless asset transfer** across platforms

As interoperability solutions become more sophisticated, they will significantly enhance the functionality of blockchain networks, enabling **cross-chain decentralized applications (dApps)**, **multi-chain DeFi protocols**, and more interconnected services across various blockchain ecosystems.

172

Summary

Technological innovations like **Layer 2 solutions**, the advent of **quantum computing**, and **blockchain interoperability** are shaping the future of blockchain technology. These emerging trends are focused on solving key challenges like **scalability**, **security**, and **fragmentation**, and have the potential to make blockchain networks more **efficient**, **secure**, and **interconnected**. As these trends continue to develop, we can expect to see **increased adoption** and **new use cases** emerge, ultimately driving the widespread integration of blockchain technology into industries worldwide.

The Social Impact of Blockchain

Blockchain technology has the potential to drive significant **social change** by promoting **justice, privacy**, and **equitable access** to technology. As a **decentralized** and **transparent** system, blockchain can fundamentally shift how individuals interact with financial, social, and political systems, paving the way for more **inclusive** and **empowered** societies. This section explores the profound impact blockchain can have on **social justice, data ownership, voting, charity**, and the **democratization** of access to resources and opportunities.

1. Blockchain's Impact on Social Justice, Privacy, and Data Ownership

One of the most powerful aspects of blockchain is its ability to **empower individuals** by giving them greater control over their personal data and financial assets, which traditionally are controlled by centralized institutions like banks, governments, and corporations. Blockchain offers several key features that could revolutionize social justice and privacy:

- **Data Ownership and Privacy**: With blockchain, individuals can take **ownership** of their own data rather than having it stored and controlled by third parties (e.g., tech companies). Blockchain's **cryptographic security** ensures that sensitive personal information is protected, giving users full control over who accesses their data and how it is shared. This could help address growing concerns around **data privacy** and misuse.
- **Social Justice and Financial Inclusion**: Blockchain has the potential to **reduce inequality** by providing access to financial services for individuals who are **unbanked** or **underbanked**, especially in regions where traditional banking systems are inaccessible. **Cryptocurrencies** and **DeFi** (Decentralized Finance) platforms allow individuals to participate in the global economy without needing to rely on traditional banking systems or face barriers to entry such as credit scores or government-issued IDs.
- **Transparent Record-Keeping**: Blockchain's immutable ledger provides a **transparent** record of transactions that cannot be altered, which can be used to track the **movement of goods** and **resources**, prevent corruption, and

expose human rights abuses. This feature is particularly valuable for initiatives aimed at ensuring **accountability** and **transparency** in government and organizations.

2. Blockchain in Voting, Charity, and Social Movements

Blockchain's transparency, security, and ability to enable decentralized systems make it an ideal technology for promoting **democracy**, **fairness**, and **accountability** in key social sectors like voting, charity, and activism.

- **Voting Systems**: Traditional voting systems are often criticized for being vulnerable to fraud, manipulation, and inefficiency. Blockchain could enable **secure, transparent, and tamper-proof voting** systems, ensuring the integrity of election results and increasing voter trust. Blockchain-based voting systems could also enable **remote voting** with strong **identity verification** measures, improving **accessibility** and **participation** in elections, particularly for marginalized communities or individuals living in remote areas.

- **Charity and Transparency**: Blockchain can greatly enhance the **transparency** and **efficiency** of charitable donations. By using blockchain, donors can track exactly where their contributions go and ensure that the funds are being used appropriately. This increases accountability and trust in charitable organizations. Blockchain's ability to provide a **clear audit trail** is particularly important for organizations working on **humanitarian** and **social justice** projects, where transparency is critical for ensuring that funds reach the intended recipients.

- **Social Movements and Activism**: Activists and social movements can use blockchain to organize and coordinate efforts in a decentralized, transparent, and **secure** manner. Blockchain can help **protect activists' identities**, prevent censorship, and track social movements and campaigns. Additionally, it can be used to create **Decentralized Autonomous Organizations (DAOs)**, which can serve as platforms for collective decision-making and coordination.

3. Democratizing Access to Financial and Technological Systems

Blockchain's ability to create **open-source**, **decentralized**, and **global networks** is a key factor in its potential to democratize access to resources and technology. It allows for the creation of systems that are **borderless**, **permissionless**, and **accessible** to anyone with an internet connection. Here's how blockchain could drive greater **democratization**:

- **Access to Financial Systems**: Blockchain-based cryptocurrencies and decentralized financial platforms (DeFi) allow individuals in developing countries or regions with poor banking infrastructure to access financial services like **savings**, **loans**, and **investments**. Without needing a traditional bank account or credit score, individuals can engage in financial transactions and wealth-building opportunities.
- **Global Digital Identity**: Blockchain technology can enable the creation of a **self-sovereign digital identity** that is both secure and verifiable. This could provide indi-

176

viduals with a **portable**, **secure** form of identification that is not reliant on government institutions, which could be especially important for **refugees, stateless individuals**, or those without access to formal identification.

- **Access to Education and Employment**: Blockchain can also help democratize access to education and employment by allowing individuals to prove their qualifications and work experience using **verified credentials** stored on the blockchain. This would help break down barriers to employment and education, particularly for individuals who may lack traditional forms of verification or face discrimination based on their background.

Summary

Blockchain has the potential to make a profound impact on social issues, including **privacy, data ownership, financial inclusion**, and **social justice**. Through innovations like **secure voting systems, transparent charity donations**, and the ability to create decentralized financial systems, blockchain can empower individuals to take control of their data and finances while increasing **trust** and **accountability**. By democratizing access to essential resources, blockchain technology is helping to bridge the digital divide and create a more inclusive world.

Preparing for the Future of Blockchain and Cryptocurrency

As blockchain technology continues to evolve and expand into new industries, it's crucial for both individuals and businesses to understand how they can **prepare** for the future of this transformative technology. Whether you're looking to stay ahead in a blockchain-driven world, explore career opportunities, or capitalize on investment and business prospects, it's essential to equip yourself with the **knowledge**, **skills**, and **resources** needed to thrive in this rapidly changing landscape.

In this section, we'll explore the various steps individuals and businesses can take to **adapt** to blockchain technology, as well as how to leverage emerging opportunities to stay competitive and relevant in an increasingly decentralized world.

1. How Individuals and Businesses Can Stay Ahead in a Blockchain-Driven World

- **Embrace Lifelong Learning**: Blockchain technology is advancing quickly, and staying up-to-date requires a commitment to **continuous learning**. Individuals should invest time in understanding the foundational concepts of blockchain, cryptocurrencies, and smart contracts, as well as keep up with the latest trends in **DeFi**, **NFTs**, **Layer 2 solutions**, and **interoperability**.

- **Adapting Business Models**: Businesses must recognize the potential of blockchain to **revolutionize industries** and consider how it can improve operational efficiencies, reduce costs, and enhance transparency. Early adoption of blockchain-based solutions can provide a competitive edge. For example, businesses can integrate blockchain for **supply chain management**, **digital payments**, **data security**, and **customer loyalty programs**.

- **Invest in Blockchain Technology**: Whether you're an individual investor or a business, **strategic investment** in blockchain and cryptocurrency projects can be a way to stay ahead. Investing in promising blockchain startups, DeFi protocols, or cryptocurrency assets can position you as an early adopter of technology that is set to grow in the coming years.

- **Collaborate and Network**: As the blockchain ecosystem grows, collaborating with industry leaders, blockchain enthusiasts, and tech innovators can provide valuable insights. Attending blockchain conferences, joining online communities, and participating in **hackathons** or **open-source projects** can help you stay connected and engaged with the blockchain ecosystem.

2. Resources for Learning and Adapting to Blockchain Technology

As blockchain and cryptocurrency are still relatively new concepts, the good news is there is an abundance of resources available for both **beginners** and **advanced learners**. These resources can help you gain the skills necessary to thrive in a blockchain-driven world:

- **Online Courses and Certifications**: Many platforms now offer online courses specifically focused on blockchain technology, crypto trading, smart contracts, and decentralized finance (DeFi). Some well-known platforms include:

- **Coursera**, **edX**, and **Udemy** offer courses from top universities and blockchain experts.
- **Certified Blockchain Developer (CBD)** and **Certified Blockchain Professional (CBP)** certifications can boost your credibility in the blockchain field.
- **Blockchain Communities**: Joining blockchain communities and forums such as **Reddit**, **BitcoinTalk**, and **Stack Exchange** can help you connect with others who are passionate about blockchain and cryptocurrency. These communities are excellent for sharing knowledge, asking questions, and discovering emerging trends.
- **Books, Podcasts, and Blogs**: Many thought leaders and industry experts regularly publish books, articles, podcasts, and blogs to help you stay informed. Some popular resources include:
- **Books** like *Blockchain Revolution* by Don and Alex Tapscott, *The Blockchain Bible*, and *Mastering Bitcoin* by Andreas M. Antonopoulos.
- **Podcasts** such as **Unchained**, **The Pomp Podcast**, and **The Bad Crypto Podcast** provide interviews with industry leaders and insight into blockchain trends.
- **Hackathons and Open-Source Projects**: Getting hands-on experience through **hackathons**, **blockchain coding challenges**, and contributing to **open-source blockchain projects** can help you understand the technology's real-world applications. Websites like **GitHub** and **Devpost** host a variety of blockchain projects and contests to get involved in.

3. How to Get Involved in the Blockchain Ecosystem

The blockchain ecosystem is vast, with numerous opportunities for individuals to **participate** and **contribute**. Here are some ways to get involved:

- **Career Paths**: Blockchain-related careers are growing rapidly across various fields, and many companies are actively seeking professionals with blockchain expertise. Some key roles include:
- **Blockchain Developer**: Developing and implementing blockchain-based solutions, smart contracts, and decentralized applications (dApps).
- **Blockchain Project Manager**: Overseeing blockchain projects, ensuring deadlines, budgets, and scope are met.
- **Crypto Analyst/Trader**: Analyzing cryptocurrency markets and trends to make investment decisions or provide financial services.
- **Blockchain Consultant**: Advising businesses on how to integrate blockchain technology into their operations.
- As blockchain technology expands, other opportunities will emerge across various sectors like **legal**, **finance**, **marketing**, and **education**.
- **Investing in Blockchain Projects**: Individuals can explore **investment opportunities** in the blockchain and cryptocurrency space through **direct investments in crypto assets**, **participation in ICOs or STOs**, or funding blockchain startups through **venture capital** or **angel investing**. Understanding how to assess projects, including evaluating their use cases, teams, and technology, is crucial to making informed decisions.

- **Building or Joining Blockchain Projects**: One of the most impactful ways to engage with the blockchain ecosystem is by **creating** or **joining** a blockchain-based project. Whether you're developing a decentralized application (dApp), launching an NFT collection, or working on a DeFi protocol, hands-on involvement in building solutions will deepen your knowledge and help you gain credibility within the community.
- **Participating in DAOs (Decentralized Autonomous Organizations)**: DAOs are organizations that operate on blockchain networks using smart contracts. By joining a DAO, individuals can participate in **decision-making processes** and contribute to the growth and direction of blockchain projects. DAOs are popular in DeFi communities, social movements, and charitable initiatives.

Summary

Preparing for the future of blockchain and cryptocurrency requires both **education** and **action**. By staying informed through continuous learning, seeking out relevant resources, and exploring career or investment opportunities, individuals and businesses can position themselves to take full advantage of the possibilities blockchain offers. The key is to embrace **innovation**, engage with the **ecosystem**, and be proactive in **adapting** to the changes blockchain will bring to the world.

Blockchain Technology, Cryptocurrencies and Your Path

Congratulations on completing your journey through the world of blockchain technology and cryptocurrencies! By now, you've gained a comprehensive understanding of how blockchain works, why cryptocurrencies are revolutionizing finance, and how this technology is shaping industries far beyond digital currencies. Whether you're an investor, a business leader, or simply a curious individual, you now have the tools to explore, adapt, and engage with these groundbreaking technologies.

In this book, we've covered a wide array of topics that have laid the foundation for your blockchain and cryptocurrency knowledge:

1. **The Basics of Blockchain and Cryptocurrencies** – We started by exploring the fundamental concepts, from decentralized ledgers to the role of cryptography in ensuring security.
2. **How Blockchain and Cryptocurrency Work in Practice** – You learned how blockchain transactions are verified, how cryptocurrencies are mined or staked, and the significance of public and private keys.

3. **The Real-World Applications of Blockchain and Cryptocurrency** – We took a deeper dive into how blockchain and crypto are transforming industries, from finance to healthcare, supply chains to voting systems.

4. **The Future of Blockchain and Cryptocurrency** – Finally, we explored the future possibilities, the challenges ahead, and how you can prepare to stay ahead in this rapidly evolving space.

By understanding these key concepts, you now have a clearer picture of how blockchain and cryptocurrency can influence your life and business, offering new opportunities, efficiencies, and ways to engage with the global economy. Whether you're looking to dive deeper into decentralized finance (DeFi), engage in tokenization and smart contracts, or explore new career paths in blockchain, this book has laid the groundwork for your next steps.

Thank You for Your Time and Commitment

I want to take a moment to sincerely **thank you** for dedicating your time to reading this book. Your commitment to learning about blockchain and cryptocurrency is a critical step toward embracing the future of technology and finance. I hope the insights shared here empower you to make informed decisions, adopt new strategies, and take advantage of the immense potential of blockchain technology.

As you continue to explore the world of cryptocurrencies and blockchain, remember that learning is a continuous journey. Stay curious, stay engaged, and keep pushing the boundaries of what's possible in this exciting and ever-evolving field.

For my next steps

As I am sure you can tell, cryptocurrencies and blockchain technology is a passion. I will continue to learn, to explore and to grow as the industry and technology matures. I expect that there will be additional future publications and resources which I will provide in the future. Stay tuned!

A Request for Your Feedback

If you found this book helpful, I would be incredibly grateful if you could take a moment to leave a review on Amazon. Your feedback not only helps me improve future editions but also assists other readers who are just starting their journey into the world of blockchain and cryptocurrencies. Simply visit the Amazon page for this book, scroll down to the "Customer Reviews" section, and share your thoughts. Your review can make a significant difference in helping others discover and benefit from the information you've gained.

Thank you once again for reading, and I wish you all the best on your blockchain and cryptocurrency journey. The future is decentralized, and you are now well-equipped to take part in it.

Stay curious, stay innovative, and most importantly, stay ahead.

Andre St Pierre

References

Antonopoulos, A. M. (2017). *Mastering Bitcoin: Unlocking digital cryptocurrencies* (2nd ed.). O'Reilly Media.

Catalini, C., & Gans, J. S. (2016). *Some Simple Economics of the Blockchain. MIT Sloan Research Paper No. 5191-16.* https://doi.org/10.2139/ssrn.2761581

Coinbase. (2024). *What is cryptocurrency?* Retrieved November 28, 2024, from https://www.coinbase.com/learn/crypto-basics/what-is-cryptocurrency

Ethereum Foundation. (2024). *What is Ethereum?* Retrieved November 28, 2024, from https://ethereum.org/en/what-is-ethereum/

Narayanan, A., Bonneau, J., Felten, E., Miller, A., & Shamir, A. (2016). *Bitcoin and cryptocurrency technologies.* Princeton University Press.

Tapscott, D., & Tapscott, A. (2016). *Blockchain revolution: How the technology behind bitcoin and other cryptocurrencies is changing the world*. Penguin.

U.S. Securities and Exchange Commission. (2024). *Framework for "investment contract" analysis of digital assets*. Retrieved from https://www.sec.gov/corpfin/framework-investment-contract-analysis-digital-assets

World Economic Forum. (2020). *Blockchain beyond the hype: A practical framework for business leaders*. World Economic Forum. https://www.weforum.org/reports/blockchain-beyond-the-hype

www.ingramcontent.com/pod-product-compliance
Lightning Source LLC
Chambersburg PA
CBHW031219050326
40689CB00009B/1397

* 9 7 8 1 0 6 9 2 9 4 0 4 3 *